This book looks at the history of our planet: how it was formed, what shaped it, and how it came to be full of living things – like you and me! Our planet is a unique and incredible place and has been around for billions of years. So dive into *The Big Earth Book* and take a rollercoaster ride around the most magical place in the whole of the universe.

The book is divided into four chapters – earth, air, fire and water. These four elements shape our world and through them, we can tell the story of planet Earth in four distinct sections. The ancient Greeks came up with the idea that everything in the world was created by one of these four elements. Although they are important, today we know that the planet and everything on it is actually made up of 118 different chemical elements (like carbon, oxygen and iron), and they are grouped together in the periodic table.

By using the ancient Greek's four classical elements, we can tell a tale about the immense power of our planet. This is a story that uses history, science, geography and the environment to explain the way our world was made, how we came to exist and what might happen in the future.

THE FAB FOUR

Look out for these four element characters throughout the book. They will provide you with extra facts and interesting information.

EARTH

THE WORD 'EARTH' COMES FROM THE ANGLO-SAXON WORD *ERDA*, AND MEANS GROUND OR SOIL. OUR PLANET IS ALSO CALLED EARTH.

AIR

AIR IS A MIXTURE OF DIFFERENT GASES THAT COVER PLANET EARTH IN A LAYER THAT REACHES UP TO 10,000 KILOMETRES (6,200 MILES) HIGH.

FIRE

FIRE IS A CHEMICAL REACTION THAT CREATES HEAT AND LIGHT. EARTH IS THE ONLY PLANET THAT WE KNOW OF WHERE FIRE EXISTS.

WATER

WATER IS EVERYWHERE! IT COVERS 71% OF OUR PLANET. MOST OF IT IS FOUND IN THE SALTY OCEANS, THE REST IS ICE AND FRESH WATER.

Words in **bold** are further explained in the glossary (pages 248–250).

EARTH

Of our four elements, the ancient Greeks believed that earth was associated with dryness, coldness and heaviness. To study this element we need to look at everything that is solid: from rocks and fossils in the ground, to soil and plants, but also human beings. We are made of the same substances as everything else on the planet.

In order to understand everything about the element earth, we need to understand how our planet works... and that's where it gets complicated. Our planet is also known as 'Earth'! To distinguish between 'earth' the element and 'Earth' the planet, we use a capital 'E' to name the planet on which we live.

HOW THE EARTH WAS FORMED

The Earth is one of eight planets that circle a giant star called the Sun. This family of planets and parent star, the Sun, is known as the Solar System. In our Solar System there are two types of planet: rocky and gassy. Or, we might call them earthy and airy! The basic difference is that on earthy, rocky planets like Earth and Mars, there is solid ground, so it is possible to land a spacecraft. Airy, gassy planets like Saturn and Jupiter don't have solid ground – they are made of **gas** for the most part. The rocky planets formed near the Sun, while larger, gassy planets formed further out, in the freezing part of the outer Solar System.

THE SWIRLING SOLAR SYSTEM

Our Solar System began forming more than 4.5 billion years ago. At first it was a giant, swirly, disc-shaped cloud. The cloud was made up of tiny **particles**, slowly swarming around the Sun. Then the force of **gravity** (which is present wherever there are particles) took effect. The gas and dust particles slowly gathered together to form clumps. The clumps became planetesimals, which are fragments of rock, dust and particles. These became small early planets which collided time and time again, gradually becoming bigger, until they formed the planets we know today, including Earth.

THE EARTH

Even though our Earth is tiny compared to the giant gas planets, it has a lot going on inside and out! It spins about 150 million kilometres (93 million miles) away from the Sun, which it moves around once a year, or about every 365 days.

Various others

Silicon

Oxygen

Magnesium

Iron

Even though we say the Earth is 'rocky', our planet is actually made up of lots of different kinds of elements, some solid and some gas. There's iron (32%), oxygen (30%), silicon (15%), magnesium (14%) and tiny amounts of lots of other less common **chemicals**.

4,600 million years ago (mya)
Gas and dust from a swirling disc clumped together to form planet Earth and the other planets in the Solar System.

4,500 mya
Heavy metals sunk to the centre of the Earth and formed its core. The outer layers cooled and compacted to form the Earth's solid crust.

4,400 mya
Volcanoes on Earth's surface released water **vapour** into the atmosphere. The water vapour cooled and fell as rain, creating the first oceans.

STRUCTURE OF THE EARTH

For many millions of years, the Earth was bombarded by comets and asteroids crashing into its crust. **Radioactive** material deep inside the Earth gave out huge waves of heat and this kept Earth **liquid** and **molten**. With all this **matter** floating around, the force of gravity was able to go to work. Gravity made the heavy, **dense** material sink to the centre of the Earth. Lighter, less dense material settled in layers above. As Earth cooled down by radiating its heat out into space, the materials inside it gradually changed from liquids to solids. Our planet was left with the solid, layered structure we have today.

THE MANTLE

The mantle is the layer of the Earth directly below the crust. The mantle is much thicker than the crust at nearly 3,000 km (1,860 mi) deep. The mantle is divided into layers and is made up mostly of silicon, oxygen and a heavier chemical, magnesium.

THE CORE

The Earth's core is mostly made of liquid iron and nickel, and has a temperature of between 5,000–6,000°C (9,000–10,800°F). The inner core at the very centre of the Earth is the hottest, and because there's so much **pressure** at this depth it is solid. The outer core is a liquid layer below the mantle.

HOW DO WE KNOW?

We know about the Earth's structure, not from digging, but from reading earthquakes. When a large earthquake happens, waves, known as seismic waves, pass through the interior of the Earth. As seismic waves travel, they bend, just as light rays bend when they pass through water. The speed of seismic waves depends on the density inside the Earth. By studying the speed we can work out what the layers inside the Earth are like, and which layers are the most dense. Read more about earthquakes on page 26.

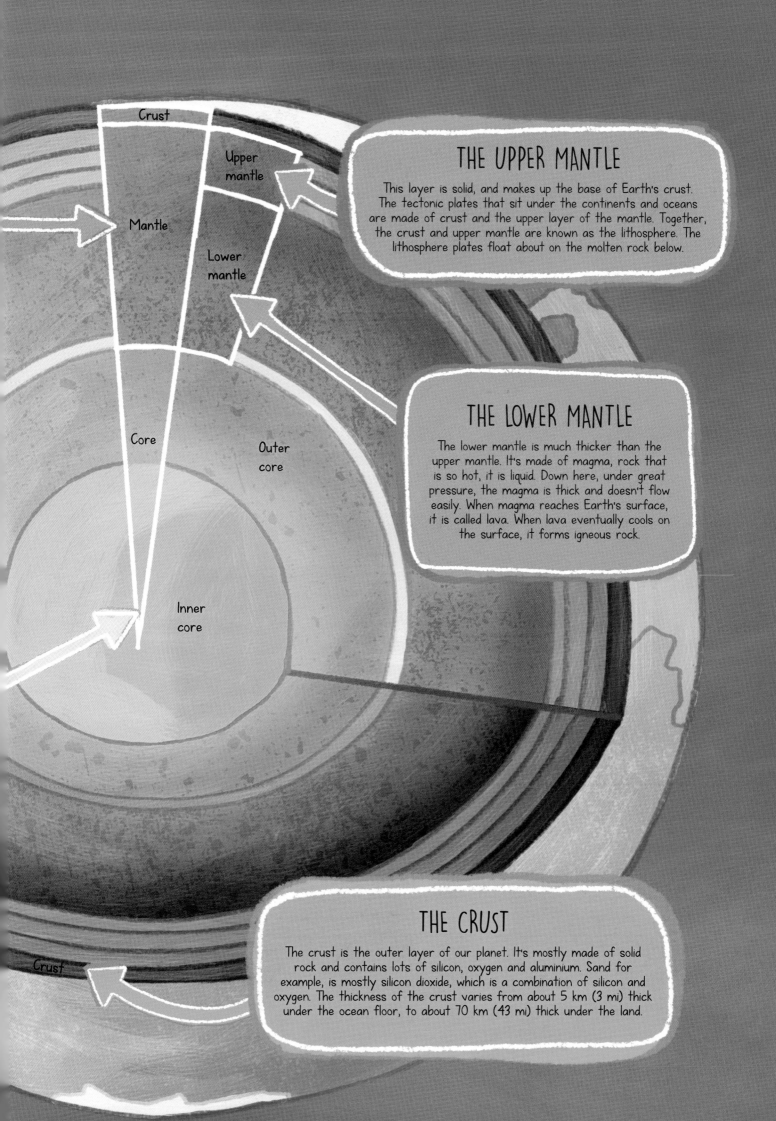

Crust

Mantle

Upper mantle

Lower mantle

Core

Outer core

Inner core

Crust

THE UPPER MANTLE

This layer is solid, and makes up the base of Earth's crust. The tectonic plates that sit under the continents and oceans are made of crust and the upper layer of the mantle. Together, the crust and upper mantle are known as the lithosphere. The lithosphere plates float about on the molten rock below.

THE LOWER MANTLE

The lower mantle is much thicker than the upper mantle. It's made of magma, rock that is so hot, it is liquid. Down here, under great pressure, the magma is thick and doesn't flow easily. When magma reaches Earth's surface, it is called lava. When lava eventually cools on the surface, it forms igneous rock.

THE CRUST

The crust is the outer layer of our planet. It's mostly made of solid rock and contains lots of silicon, oxygen and aluminium. Sand for example, is mostly silicon dioxide, which is a combination of silicon and oxygen. The thickness of the crust varies from about 5 km (3 mi) thick under the ocean floor, to about 70 km (43 mi) thick under the land.

EVOLVING EARTH

Have you ever looked at a map of the world and noticed that the east coast of South America is almost a perfect jigsaw fit with the west coast of Africa? In 1912, a German scientist called Alfred Wegener noticed this jigsaw fit too. Alfred wondered, if he created a film in his mind and made the areas of land, or the continents, move across the seas, back to where they seem to have come from – what would the Earth have looked like? Alfred's answer was that the continents must have been joined together in one supercontinent which he named Pangea. To help them understand conditions on Earth millions of years ago, scientists use a geological timescale to understand the order in which things happened.

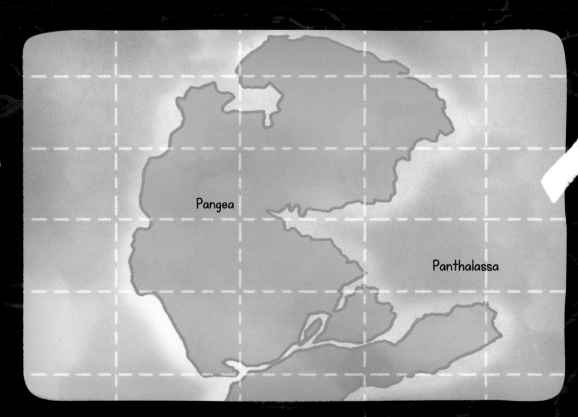

PERMIAN, 225 MYA

Before Pangea formed as a supercontinent, it had existed as separate continents that drifted together. Pangea existed for about 100 million years before it began to divide up again.

Pangea

Panthalassa

PANGEA

Africa

South America

Range of Mesosaurus fossils

Scientists researching Pangea discovered that similar rocks and fossils could be found in countries that are now separated by vast oceans. For example, fossils of Mesosaurus, a reptile that lived hundreds of millions of years ago, were found in southern South America and southern Africa. Alfred was convinced that the supercontinent of Pangea must have been surrounded by just one ocean, which he called Panthalassa.

DRIFT OR PLATES?

Scientists liked Alfred's idea of Pangea, but they weren't so keen on his suggestion that the continents just drifted apart. The idea of continental drift was replaced with the discovery of the Earth's plates. These plates are called tectonic plates and some are more than 200 km (120 mi) thick). They are slabs of the Earth's crust and upper mantle which together make the lithosphere. The lithosphere floats above the magma in the lower mantle below. It's the movement of the plates that explains the shape and position of the continents.

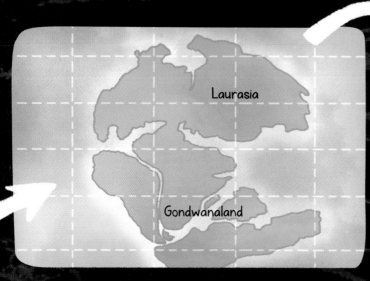

TRIASSIC, 200 MYA

Gradually, Pangea broke up into two large land masses. One is known as Laurasia, and is roughly today's Northern Hemisphere. The other land mass is Gondwanaland, and is approximately today's Southern Hemisphere.

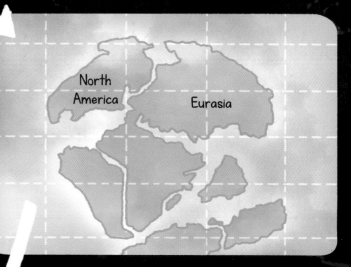

JURASSIC, 150 MYA

During the Jurassic Period, Laurasia slowly split into North America and Eurasia.

CRETACEOUS, 65 MYA

During the Cretaceous Period, Gondwanaland split into Africa, Antarctica, Australia and South America. Some of the land masses rotated slightly as they separated.

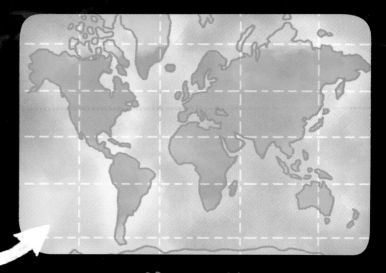

PRESENT DAY

The continents settled into the map of the world as we know it. But for how long? Scientists believe Africa is moving towards southern Europe, and Australia will collide with Southeast Asia. This will make a new supercontinent – but it won't happen for another 250 million years!

PLATE TECTONICS

Imagine the surface of Earth as a jigsaw puzzle. Those puzzle pieces of land have somehow moved across the globe from the time of the Pangea land mass. We know that the land sits on plates. And we know that the plates, which vary in thickness, are made of parts of the lithosphere, which floats on top of the Earth's lower mantle. But what evidence is there to tell us that all of this is true? The research into this is called plate tectonics.

PATTERNS UNDER THE OCEAN

The rocks which make up the ocean's crust have a pattern in them. This pattern was locked into the rocks when they formed. But the pattern is not always the same. Some layers of rock are different to others and this shows that the rock, and the continents, have moved.

When scientists mapped the ocean floor, they found it was much younger than they expected. They also found mountain ranges on the ocean floor! Either side of the mountain ranges, the pattern within the rock was the same.

From studying patterns in the rocks and the underwater mountains, scientists came up with the idea of seafloor spreading. This is when land masses move slightly creating cracks where magma can pour out of the crust and separate the sea floor! The magma is making new seabed, which explains why it looks so young. As new sea floor is made, old sea floor disappears into trenches, elsewhere in the Earth's crust!

EVIDENCE OF MOVEMENT

When scientists started looking for fossils in the 19th century, they noticed something quite curious. The fossils showed that there were creatures on Earth that no longer existed, and those creatures lived far from where the fossils were found. One fossil of an extinct sea creature was found on top of a mountain, in the middle of a desert! How did rock containing the fossils move from one part of the globe to another? The rock with the fossil must have moved down into the Earth's crust at some point, and then reappeared when this bit of crust was pushed up to form a new mountain.

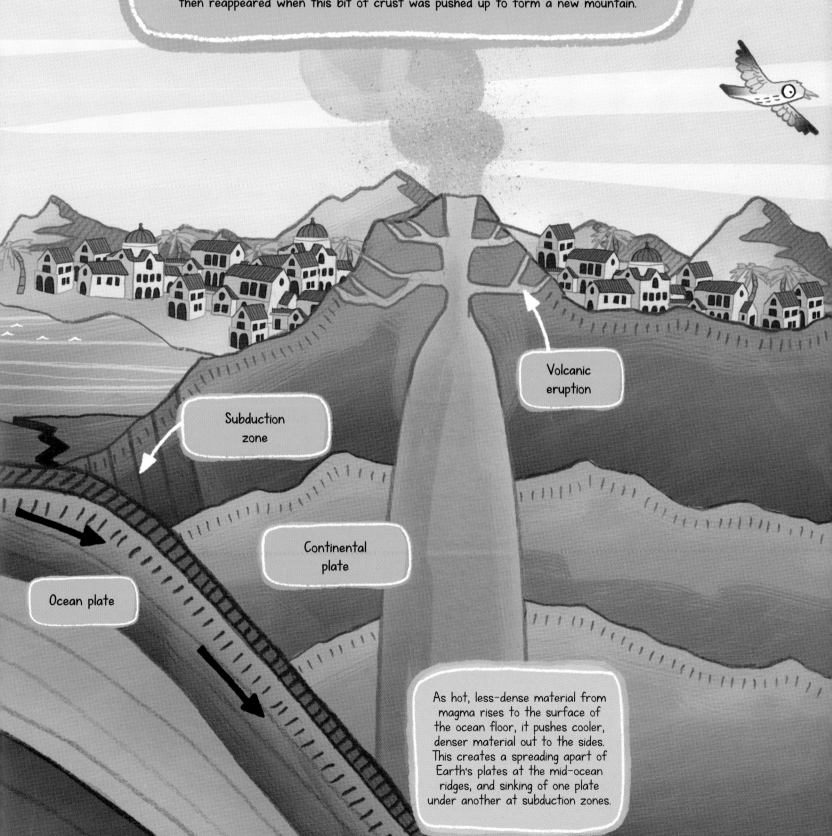

Volcanic eruption

Subduction zone

Continental plate

Ocean plate

As hot, less-dense material from magma rises to the surface of the ocean floor, it pushes cooler, denser material out to the sides. This creates a spreading apart of Earth's plates at the mid-ocean ridges, and sinking of one plate under another at subduction zones.

ROCKS!

Imagine being in a desert on a boiling hot day. For many miles, as far as your eye can see, there's just dune after dune of sweeping sand. Imagine reaching down, hands cupped, and gathering up the golden sand. The entire desert is made only of these tiny grains. If all those grains were squished tightly together, under great pressure, they would interlock to make rock. There are three main kinds of rock: sedimentary, igneous and metamorphic.

IGNEOUS ROCKS

The inside of planet Earth is hot enough to melt rocks into a molten, liquid form known as magma. When magma rises to the Earth's surface and pours out, it becomes lava. When lava cools and settles, it becomes solid igneous rock. Igneous rock is made of interlocking crystals, set out in a random pattern. If the magma cools quickly, the crystals are small, such as in basalt rock. If lava solidifies slowly, then the crystals are bigger, as in granite rock.

METAMORPHIC ROCKS

Metamorphic rocks are made from sedimentary or igneous rocks, which have been changed (or metamorphosed) due to heat or pressure. Movement in the Earth makes rocks hot, or puts them under great pressure. The rocks don't melt in these conditions but their chemical crystals change. Metamorphic rocks can be made when sedimentary rocks come close to molten rock, or magma. The metamorphic rocks heat up and change structure!

5. Some sedimentary rocks melt and become magma. The magma reforms as igneous rock.

6. When sedimentary and igneous rocks are exposed to heat and pressure, they change into metamorphic rock.

THE ROCK CYCLE

All three types of rock are constantly changing and moving in what is known as the rock cycle.

1. **Weathering** by water and wind causes rocks on land to gradually wear away.

2. Small broken pieces of rock are carried away by water and worn down into smaller grains.

3. The grains of rock are deposited in lakes and seas, and build up to form layers of sediment.

4. The layers of sediment are compressed and become sedimentary rock.

SEDIMENTARY ROCKS

When grains of rock are broken off from other rocks, the grains are carried along in rivers to lakes or out to sea. The grains of rock and sand drift down to the bottom of the water and settle in layers, known as sediments. The weight of all the new sediments on top squashes the sediments at the bottom. Water is squeezed out and crystals are formed. The crystals create a kind of glue that binds the rock together, creating sedimentary rock.

LAYERS OF SOIL

There's a rainbow under your feet! Dig down through the layers of soil and you'll find bands of earth as red as blood, and others as black as coal. Some layers are lemon yellow, while others are white as snow. The colours in the soil are created by all sorts of materials. **Minerals** and many living creatures are in the mix, plus water, air and organic matter such as plants. Soil is the surface of the land on our planet. It's sometimes called the 'skin of the Earth', and is very important for life on our planet.

4. Soil acts as a home for many animals such as groundhogs, moles and mice, and **organisms** like fungi and bacteria.

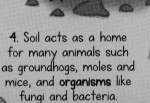

SOIL HORIZONS

Each type of soil has its own character. Dig down deep, and you'll find that the soil is made of different bands known as horizons. Together, the horizons form a soil profile, which tells a tale about the life of the soil wherever you are on Earth.

A HORIZON - TOPSOIL

Topsoil is made from **organic matter** and minerals. This horizon is the layer where most plants and animals live.

D HORIZON - BEDROCK

The bedrock horizon is made up of a large solid mass of rock, such as granite, basalt, quartzite, limestone or sandstone.

THE SEVEN FUNCTIONS OF SOIL

Soil has seven major roles to play on planet Earth.

1. Soil affects the air around it by giving out and absorbing gases such as carbon dioxide, water vapour and methane.

2. Soil is used by humans for buildings, roads and dams.

3. Soil soaks up, holds, changes and purifies most of the water found on land.

5. Soil provides the nutrients that plants need for growth.

6. Soil acts as a filter to cleanse water before it seeps into rocks.

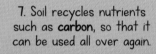

7. Soil recycles nutrients such as **carbon**, so that it can be used all over again.

O HORIZON - ORGANIC

This is mostly organic material, such as rotting leaves. Horizon O can be thick, thin or completely absent in soils.

B HORIZON - SUBSOIL

This horizon is mostly clay and iron. It is rich in minerals and organic material that have moved down from the horizons above.

C HORIZON - PARENT MATERIAL

Horizon C is formed of large rocks. This horizon is called the parent material. When small bits of large rocks break off they move upwards and form the horizons above.

IN A SINGLE TEASPOON OF HEALTHY SOIL YOU WILL FIND SEVERAL HUNDRED MILLION **BACTERIA!**

LIVING EARTH

The surface of planet Earth sits on plates that move. Every now and then we get a glimpse into what lies under the plates as gaps between them reveal pools of lava (magma that has reached the Earth's surface). The heat given off by this magma under the surface is what causes the movement of the plates. And the movement of the plates is what makes Earth alive with earthquakes, volcanoes and geothermal energy! We'll discover more about lava and volcanoes on pages 28–29.

Crack in the plate

Plate edges

Plate edges

HOT PLATES

When a liquid heats up, the particles in it are organised and divided into a series of zones or patterns. In each zone, hot material rises up through the middle and, when it is cooled by the air above, it falls back down around the sides of the zone. This is called convection. Deep inside the Earth, molten magma rises from the core, heating and moving the mantle, which rises up towards the Earth's crust. There, magma begins to cool and spreads sideways. Once cooled, it sinks and creates the edge of a plate. This movement is what divides the Earth's crust into plates that look like jigsaw pieces.

A series of cracks encircling the Pacific Ocean floor is known as the Ring of Fire. It is a fiery reminder of what is below Earth's surface.

Perbuatan, Krakatoa, Indonesia

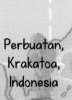

INDIA–AUSTRALIAN PLATE

The tectonic plates of the world were mapped in the second half of the 20th century.

PACIFIC PLATE

Plate movement is much too slow for us to notice. The Earth's plates only move up to 15 centimetres (6 inches) per year. That means it takes millions of years for continents to move and mountains to form.

MAJOR AND MINOR PLATES

Heat from the Earth's core shapes our world and splits the planet's surface into seven major plates and eight minor plates. The seven major plates are the African, Antarctic, Eurasian, North American, South American, India-Australian and Pacific plates. Where plates meet, mountains, rift valleys, volcanoes and earthquakes are more likely to occur. Read on through the next few pages to find out more about them.

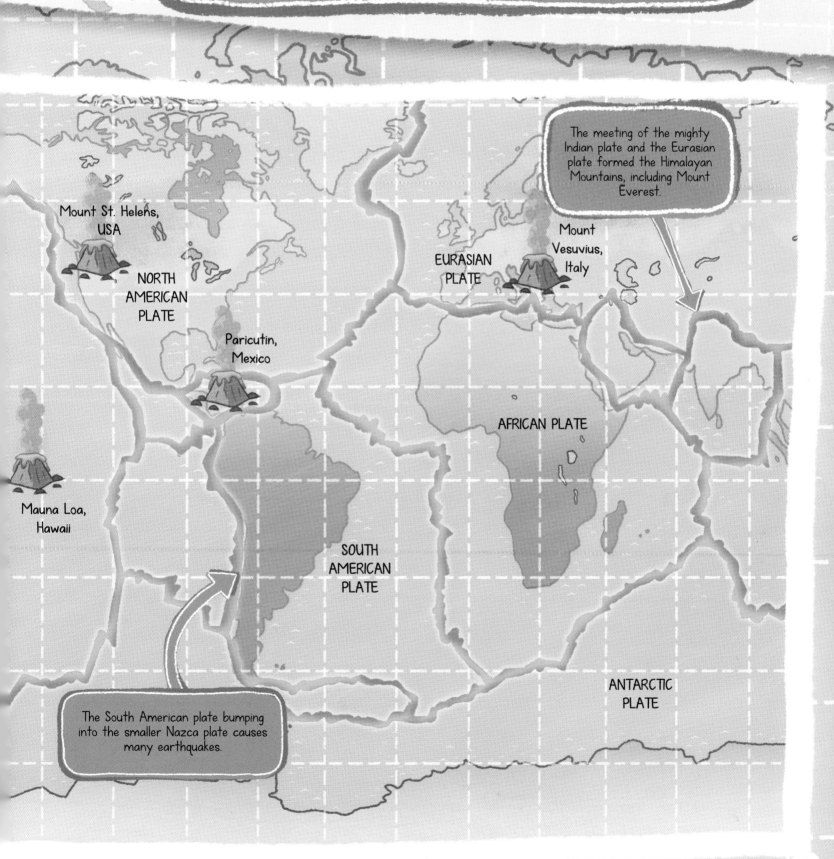

The meeting of the mighty Indian plate and the Eurasian plate formed the Himalayan Mountains, including Mount Everest.

Mount St. Helens, USA

NORTH AMERICAN PLATE

Paricutin, Mexico

Mauna Loa, Hawaii

SOUTH AMERICAN PLATE

EURASIAN PLATE

Mount Vesuvius, Italy

AFRICAN PLATE

ANTARCTIC PLATE

The South American plate bumping into the smaller Nazca plate causes many earthquakes.

FAULTS AND BOUNDARIES

The Earth's crust is divided into plates that fit together like a giant jigsaw puzzle. In some places where the plates meet there are cracks known as fault lines. Dramatic volcanoes and earthquakes mostly happen along these fault lines because these are places where the Earth's surface is most active. It is the movement between the plate boundaries that causes the activity.

DIVERGENT BOUNDARIES

A divergent boundary, or 'spreading zone', is where two plates are pushed apart as magma rises up to the surface to create new crust. These boundaries are most often found in the middle of the ocean, but if the boundary is on land, it's known as a rift. The East African Rift is a good example – it's where the main African plate is splitting apart into two plates: the Somali plate and the Nubian plate. But don't get too excited! The plates are speeding along at only 7 millimetres (0.3 in) per year. You'll have to wait millions of years to see a rupture in the surface happen.

PLATE BOUNDARIES

Fault lines circle the globe and surround whole continents, some stretching for 70,000 km (43,500 mi). Along each fault line there are three types of boundary: divergent, transform and convergent. The movement of plates at these boundaries is responsible for creating rift valleys, volcanoes, mountains and earthquakes. At Thingvellir National Park in Iceland, two divergent plates are slowly pulling apart. A rift valley has formed and in some places it's possible to walk between the two plates.

CONVERGENT BOUNDARIES

This boundary is where two plates push together. Most often a slab of ocean floor meets a continent. Because the ocean plate is heavier, it sinks beneath the continent in a process called subduction. When two continental plates meet, very little subduction occurs. Instead, the plates crumple and fold to create valleys, ridges and high mountain ranges. That's why you find many mountains and volcanoes at these boundaries, and lots of earthquakes too. The Himalayas were formed along two convergent plates.

TRANSFORM BOUNDARIES

A transform boundary is where two plates slide past each other, in opposite directions. The plates sometimes get stuck and that leads to the build-up of pressure. When the pressure is finally released, the plates move suddenly, causing an earthquake. The most famous transform boundary in the world is the San Andreas fault in California, USA. At this boundary there are a lot of earthquakes. One side of the state of California is slowly moving northwards. This means that the city of Los Angeles will slowly creep up towards San Francisco and the cities will be side-by-side in around 10 million years time!

EARTHQUAKES

Fault lines are home to a famous and deadly force created by our mighty planet - earthquakes! An earthquake is a vibration that travels through the Earth's crust. They can be triggered by volcanic eruptions and asteroid impacts, but most quakes are caused by movements in the Earth's plates. Convergent and transform plate boundaries push rocks together, causing **friction**. When the friction builds up, the rocks become locked, so they no longer slide past each other. The pressure builds up energy until the lock suddenly gives way, and the rock snaps forward, shaking the ground. Turn to page 236 to read about how earthquakes can trigger tsunamis.

26TH JANUARY 1700 NORTHWEST COAST OF NORTH AMERICA

Native Americans living near Vancouver Island tell of how a large community on the coast was entirely wiped out by this earthquake in 1700. Stories also tell how people felt the after-effects as far away as Japan – on the other side of the Pacific Ocean!

LIVING ON FAULT LINES

Since the dawn of **civilisation**, people have often set up home by fault lines. This is because the soil in these areas is full of **nutrients** and is excellent for growing crops. But living by fault lines is dangerous and there is always the risk of an earthquake happening. Modern societies living on fault lines take time to educate people about what to do if an earthquake hits. In Japan, school children are taught to shelter under their desks and hold on to the legs until the quake is over.

These schoolchildren are taking part in an earthquake drill in Japan.

11TH JANUARY 1693 SICILY, ITALY

This huge earthquake is thought to be the most powerful in Italian history. It destroyed more than 70 towns and cities in southern Italy, causing the death of 60,000 people.

FAMOUS EARTHQUAKES

22ND MAY 1960
CHILE

The world's most powerful quake struck in southern Chile, killing 4,485 people. A day later the Puyehue volcano in Chile's lake district spewed ash 6,000 m (19,500 ft) into the air in an eruption that lasted for several weeks.

12TH JANUARY 2010
PORT-AU-PRINCE, HAITI

The main shock was followed by at least 52 aftershocks which continued for 12 days. Aftershocks happen when the initial earthquake passes some of its energy onto nearby rocks which then start to move and build friction. The quake killed 316,000 people, injuring another 300,000 and made over 1 million people homeless

1ST NOVEMBER 1755
LISBON, PORTUGAL

The 'Great Lisbon Earthquake' almost totally destroyed the Portuguese capital in 1755, and led to the deaths of one quarter of the city's people. The shock was felt in north Africa, France and northern Italy, too.

EARTHQUAKE ENGINEERING

Engineers today work hard to create modern buildings and bridges that are designed to withstand earthquakes. These structures try to ride the waves of the most fearsome shocks and remain intact once the quaking has stopped. Engineering like this has a long history. The Hagia Sophia in Istanbul, Turkey, was built in AD 537. Twenty years after it was completed, the dome collapsed when an earthquake hit the city. When it was rebuilt, on a smaller scale, builders revised the design to be able to cope with earthquakes and so the Hagia Sophia still stands to this day.

VOLCANOES

A volcano is an opening in the Earth's surface where magma from the lower mantle forces its way up to the surface and explodes in an eruption. Volcanic ash (tiny rock and mineral particles), steam and gases also escape and the event can be very dramatic. There are three types of volcano: stratovolcanoes, shield volcanoes and cinder cone volcanoes. Large volcanic eruptions can create whole islands from their lava, and destroy them too! When a volcano erupted on the island of Santorini in Greece around 1500 BC, the lava that flowed out left an enormous hole under the island. The middle of the island collapsed into the sea, leaving the steep-sided, crescent-shaped island that is there today.

SHIELD VOLCANOES

Shield volcanoes are the largest type. The lava flows over great distances, and when it cools, it forms a thin but wide dome, which looks a little like a shield. They may be big, but shield volcanoes erupt quite gently, so tourists can often watch the lava flow out in places like Hawaii.

STRATOVOLCANOES

This is the most common type of volcano and it has the recognisable dome shape. This is because when lava cools in the air, it solidifies around the opening. Stratovolcanoes often come in groups, lined up in a chain. These volcanoes have thicker and stickier lava than others and because of this, the pressure that builds before an eruption is huge.

CINDER CONE VOLCANOES

The smallest type of volcano is called a cinder cone. This volcano forms when thin magma is forced into the air during an eruption. It solidifies and falls back to Earth in pieces known as 'cinders'. In time, the cinders pile up, creating a cone shaped volcano. The Parícutin volcano is a cinder cone volcano in Mexico. It first erupted out of a small crack in the ground in 1943. In just nine years, it turned a flat field into a 424-metre (1,391-foot) high cinder cone volcano and buried two villages in the process.

ERUPTION!

Volcanoes can be found almost everywhere on the Earth – Australia is the only continent without an active one. After a dramatic explosion, volcanoes pose a deadly risk to humans and animals. Fast-moving, burning-hot lava may cover the local area, killing and destroying everything in its path and causing permanent damage. Thick ash can poison animals and cause breathing problems in humans. And if the volcano is located near a glacier, the melting ice from the heat of the eruption may cause flooding. Here are four volcanoes that made some of the most famous blasts in history.

MOUNT PELÉE
MARTINIQUE, CARIBBEAN SEA, 8TH MAY 1902

Eyewitness accounts say that just before this eruption in the Caribbean, insects of all shapes and sizes appeared. Yellow ants and big, black centipedes crawled down the lush-covered slopes of Mount Pelée, sensing an eruption. Then snakes slowly slithered down the volcano's sides. Finally the explosion happened and Mount Pelée blew its top.
A huge cloud of glowing gas was forced out at more than 160 km/h (100 mph). Three minutes later almost all of the people in the local town St Pierre were buried. Only one person survived – Auguste Ciparis, who was a prisoner in the city's dungeon.

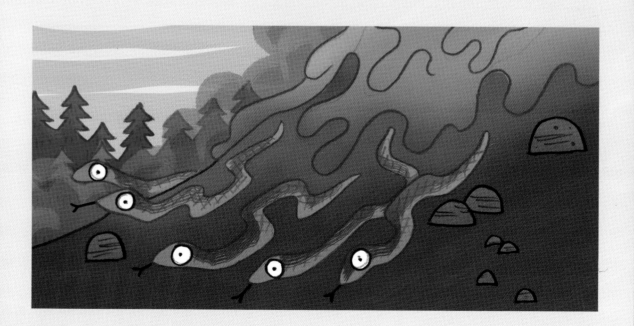

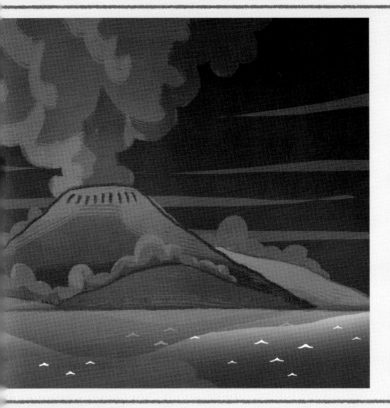

PERBUATAN
KRAKATOA ISLAND, INDONESIA, 26TH AUGUST 1883

Perbuatan and two other volcanoes created the loudest volcanic explosion in history. The sound of Krakatoa erupting was reportedly heard 4,800 km (3,000 mi) away. The Perbuatan volcano first blew up and then, on the following day, collapsed in four gigantic explosions. The shockwaves were felt around the world. Perhaps as many as 100,000 people died in the explosion, or drowned in the enormous tsunamis unleashed by the volcano's collapse. The volcanic dust flew 80 km (50 mi) into the Earth's atmosphere, creating a curtain above the globe that caused chaotic weather and scarlet sunsets. In London, the sky was so fiery red that people called out fire engines.

TAMBORA
SUMBAWA ISLAND, INDONESIA, 10TH APRIL 1815

The largest eruption ever recorded happened in Indonesia. The volcano had shown little sign of life for 1,000 years and local people thought the 4,300 m (14,100 ft) high volcano was extinct. But in 1815 it started rumbling. And on 5th April, a cloud of ash exploded 30 km (18.5 mi) into the sky. Then, after five days of calm, a colossal eruption launched a towering column of hot ash and scalding gas up to the edge of space itself. All this fell back down to Earth in the following days and weeks, causing strange weather across the world and even climate change that caused food shortages across the Northern Hemisphere the following year.

MOUNT VESUVIUS
POMPEII, ITALY, 24TH AUGUST AD 79

The day before this eruption, the Romans had celebrated Vulcanalia – a festival celebrating the god of fire. The following day, a volcanic explosion was recorded by one single survivor, a Roman senator named Pliny the Younger. Pliny witnessed a cloud of hot ash being blasted from Mount Vesuvius, 32 km (20 mi) into the sky. Then gravity took over and the cloud began to fall back to Earth, raining toxic gas on the town and its people, and burying them in ash 3 m (9 ft) deep. It happened so quickly that the city and bodies were perfectly preserved until the city was uncovered in 1748.

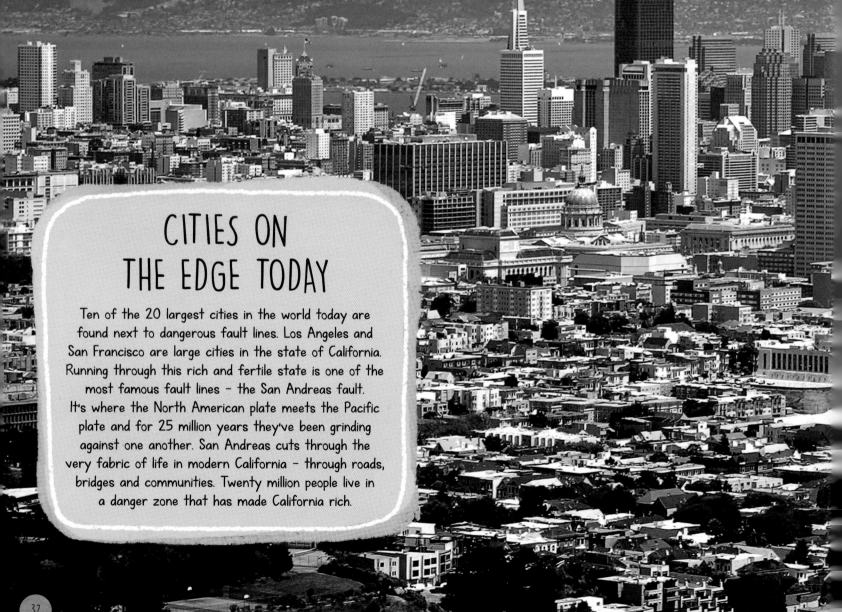

LIVING WITH THE LANDSCAPE

Despite the danger of living near volcanoes and earthquakes, 11 of the 13 most important ancient civilisations built their cities close to plate boundaries. This is because people needed access to the resources like **fertile** soil as well as the metals and minerals offered up by the rich ground. Even today, many of the world's largest cities, such as San Francisco in the USA, are located next to potentially life-threatening fault lines.

CITIES ON THE EDGE TODAY

Ten of the 20 largest cities in the world today are found next to dangerous fault lines. Los Angeles and San Francisco are large cities in the state of California. Running through this rich and fertile state is one of the most famous fault lines – the San Andreas fault. It's where the North American plate meets the Pacific plate and for 25 million years they've been grinding against one another. San Andreas cuts through the very fabric of life in modern California – through roads, bridges and communities. Twenty million people live in a danger zone that has made California rich.

COSY-UP TO A FAULT LINE

Making your home along a fault line isn't necessarily a recipe for disaster. This map shows the 13 most important civilisations in history and the locations of their major cities. Only the Chinese are far from a fault.

1. Etruscan
(Tarquinia and Veil)

2. Roman (Rome)

3. Greek (Corinth) and
Mycenaean (Mycenae)

4. Minoan (Knossos)

5. S-W Asian (Tyre)

6. S-W Asian (Jerusalem)

7. Assyrian (Nineveh)

8. Mesopotamian (Ur-Uruk)

9. Persian (Susa)

10. Indus (Mohenjo-Daro)

11. Aryan India (Hastinapura)

12. Egyptian (Memphis)

13. Chinese (Zhengahou)

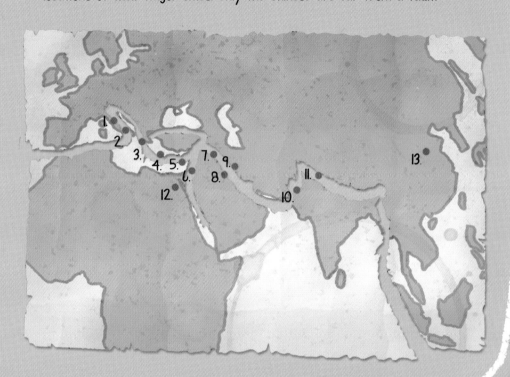

CALIFORNIA

California is one of the richest farming regions in the whole of America. When the California gold rush happened in 1848, it was because activity along the fault line forced gold up to the surface. The region is rich with oil too, and is accessible because the fault split rocks deep underground and forced oil up close to the surface where it is easy to drill wells. Maths boffins have done their homework: the next major earthquake along the San Andreas fault will cause around $250 billion worth of damage, just as the earthquake in October 1989 did. However it's worth the risk as the state also earns around $100 billion every year directly because of the proceeds from the fault's riches!

GEOTHERMAL

Volcanic hotspots aren't all bad news and scientists are learning how to tap into their power using geothermal energy. This is energy that is drawn from heat coming from deep inside the Earth and it occurs in areas where there is volcanic activity. Here, water is heated underground. When it reaches the air, the boiling water turns to steam and shoots up out of the ground in a spectacle known as a **geyser**. Where there's heat, there's energy and scientists are learning how to use this geothermal energy to power modern life.

A geyser can blow thousands of litres of boiling steam hundreds of metres in the air.

HELL'S GATE

One famous geothermal spot is 'Hell's Gate' in Rotorua, New Zealand. Here, there are boiling pools of water, mud volcanoes, sulphurous lakes and steaming cliffs alongside cold water ponds and falls. The air smells of rotten eggs due to the sulphur gases released from deep underground.

GEOTHERMAL HOTSPOTS

There are active hotspots around the world which hold lots of potential energy reserves. The areas in red on the map are hot temperature zones. Scientists in North America, Europe, Asia and Africa have begun developing geothermal energy systems following Iceland's lead, as geothermal is one of the clean energy options for the future. Ongoing projects are marked by a yellow dot – is there one near where you live?

Other pools of water may be nice and warm, but not boiling, so it is safe for people to bathe in them.

Boiling and steaming water in geothermal pools reaches 95.5°C (204°F)!

Boiling mud pool

Different types of bacteria living in the hot water turn it different colours.

THE GEOTHERMAL ISLAND!

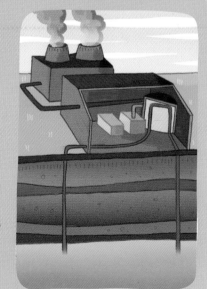

The true experts of geothermal energy are the people of Iceland. This large island sits on top of the Mid-Atlantic Ridge which is an active boundary between the North American and Eurasian tectonic plates. Volcanic activity occurs every day in Iceland, with large eruptions happening twice or more every decade. Geothermal energy is tapped by drilling down into the ground and when a steam source is found, it is used to power turbines and generate electricity. The Icelandic people are able to meet more than 60% of their energy needs using geothermal energy.

HUMANS IN THE STONE AGE

To understand human civilisation, you have to go far back in time, before the ancient Romans or Egyptians, and deep in what is called **prehistory**. The Stone Age is the age of early humans and it is the first of the three-age system that scientists use to tell the tale of the history of humans. It is followed by the Iron Age and the Bronze Age.

TIMELINE OF HUMANS ON EARTH

10 mya
Our early human **ancestors** roam the Earth.

6 mya
Human-like apes develop.

4 mya
Australopithecus marks the start of human ancestors walking mainly on two legs.

THE FIRST HUMANS

Scientists believe the first humans lived in the East African Rift Valley, a place where two divergent tectonic plates meet. The rift is a massive tear in the Earth's crust, thousands of miles long, stretching from Ethiopia to Mozambique. The space created by the tear forms a valley which is protected from harsh weather and creates good living conditions. The first humans lived along this valley, moving down into southern Africa, north to the River Nile and east into the vast grasslands of Asia. We know this because the earliest human fossils and the oldest Stone Age tools have been found here.

HUMAN DEVELOPMENT

Modern humans (like us) are scientifically named Homo sapiens (meaning 'wise man'). But our early human ancestors, who existed before Homo sapiens, have different names as they developed over time into intelligent creatures who learnt how to make and use stone tools to survive. This development took place over the entire Stone Age period which began around 2.8 million years ago.

200,000 years ago
Homo sapiens ('wise man') appears and is what we know as a modern human.

1.4 mya
This date marks the earliest use of fire by our human ancestors.

2.8 mya
Homo habilis ('able man') appears and makes the earliest known stone tools.

1.8 mya
Homo erectus ('upright man') appears.

LOOKING GOOD

Scientists believe that Homo sapiens were less primitive than Neanderthals. They were taller and more skilled and there is evidence that these early ancestors of ours liked to decorate themselves! They painted their faces and bodies with a yellow and red mineral called ochre.

0.25 mya
Homo neanderthalensis ('Neanderthal man') appears. This is a different species to Homo sapiens and became extinct 40,000 years ago.

3 mya   2 mya   1 mya   Today

LIFE IN THE STONE AGE

For many prehistoric peoples during the Stone Age, home was a cave in the rocks. The cave gave our ancestors shelter from the cold and protection from **predators**. Once they'd learnt how to create fire, they could also huddle around a campfire for warmth. By the end of the Stone Age, modern humans (Homo sapiens) roamed the land much more and so didn't create permanent cave settlements. Instead, they built makeshift shelters out in the open air using leaves and branches.

STONE TOOLS

Early humans first made tools by taking stones and chipping them with 'hammers' made of bone or rock to create sharp edges. Using leather straps made from animal skins, they tied the sharpened stone to a stick to make a handle. Over thousands of years, Homo sapiens became more and more skilled at making stone tools and they created axes, knives and spears, all mounted on wooden handles.

OLDUVAI STONE

The Olduvai stone was discovered at Olduvai in the East African Rift Valley in Africa and is thought to be around 2 million years old. It is one of the earliest tools ever made by humans. The stone could be used for chopping bones, plants and wood. The discovery of the stone helped prove that our human ancestors first evolved in Africa.

ROCK ART

Many thousands of years ago, Homo sapiens painted on the stone walls of caves. The paintings were often of hunting scenes, showing great animals like the rhinoceros, bison and horse. By mixing earth with clay, Homo sapiens made the colours red, yellow and brown, while coal was used to create black. We know early humans must have had sharp eyesight and strong hands in order to hunt, but rock art is evidence that early humans were also creative and thought about the world in which they lived.

THE CREATIVE WAY HUMANS MAKE AND USE TOOLS IS WHAT MAKES US DIFFERENT TO ANIMALS. SCIENTISTS ARE CONTINUALLY FINDING MORE EVIDENCE THAT USING TOOLS GREATLY INFLUENCED THE WAY WE **EVOLVED**.

HUMAN SIGNATURE

Cueva de las Manos (Spanish for Cave of Hands), in Argentina, shows handprints stencilled on to the cave walls from almost 10,000 years ago. People blew colour onto their outstretched hands.

THE CAVES AT LASCAUX

One of the best examples of cave art is found in caves at Lascaux, in France. The Stone Age art in the caves is around 17,500 years old. The paintings are mainly of large animals, most of which we know lived in France because of the fossil evidence that has been found there.

HUNTER-GATHERERS

Where do you go to get your meat and vegetables? The supermarket no doubt! In the Stone Age, our ancestors had to find and prepare food themselves. If they wanted to eat meat, they had to kill the animal. If they wanted a particular plant, they had to look far and wide to find it. It was hard work hunting and gathering by hand so we can understand why Stone-Age tools became so useful.

THE HUNT

During the Stone Age, Homo sapiens hunted woolly mammoth, reindeer and buffalo. Over time, prehistoric people made a very important discovery: that co-operation between people made it easier to hunt animals. Homo sapiens found that there is power in numbers – the more people involved in the hunt, the better it went! This was especially true if they planned a hunt carefully. Although stone weapons were still crucial, planning was more important than sheer force. The hunt must have been very exciting and important, as prehistoric people made it the main theme for many cave paintings.

THE STONE AGE DIET

Meat wasn't the only thing on the Stone Age menu. Prehistoric people, such as Homo sapiens and Neanderthals, also foraged for fruit, nuts, seeds, roots and mushrooms. A group of people gathering plant-based foods across a wide area were able to find much more than one person searching by themselves, so these early people learnt to work together. Our ancestors were also excellent fishermen. Nets made of animal hide were used to catch fish, and stone axes were used to make boats out of tree trunks.

HUNTER–GATHERERS TODAY

Some people, like the Masai in east Africa, still live the hunter-gatherer lifestyle today. In 2013, it was estimated there were more than 100 such tribes around the world, most of them living in the dense forests of South America, Africa and New Guinea. Many have had little to no contact with the modern world.

FARMING

Imagine you and your family have always been Stone Age hunter-gatherers and have relied mostly on meat and the hunt to survive. If you've been successful you will have a growing number of family members, but that means less meat to go around. And what if the animals you hunt start falling in numbers too? Or perhaps the climate begins to turn icy, such as when the Earth had its last **Ice Age**, between 110,000 and 12,000 years ago. If there are no animals to hunt, there's little chance your family will survive. Suddenly your hunter-gatherer skills are useless.

CULTURE CHANGE

Evidence shows us that Stone Age people consciously made a change from hunting and gathering to farming around 12,500 years ago. In a number of different places across the globe, people began to grow their own crops and look after animals. This change sounds quite simple but it is believed to have led to the most important developments in human history such as writing and mathematics (as farmers had to count and take note of their stock).

STONE BUILDINGS

Advanced Stone Age people built stone buildings and monuments all over the world, especially tombs for their dead. One of the most famous ritual stone monuments is Stonehenge, in the UK, constructed between 3000 and 2000 BC. Stonehenge is a ring of huge standing stones. Today, we are still trying to understand exactly why they were carried there and what they were for.

THE FERTILE CRESCENT

The Fertile Crescent region of south-west Asia was one of the first places in the world where people started farming. The climate there has a long, dry season, and a short season of rain. Scientists believe that plants such as wheat and barley grew naturally in the area and were relatively easy to farm. It was a natural progression for our ancestors to move from hunter-gathering, to farming in this part of the world.

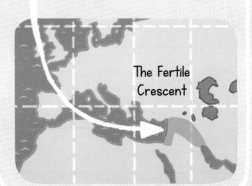

The Fertile Crescent

THE NEW STONE AGE

The period between the first instance of farming and the first cities is known as the New Stone Age (or Neolithic Period). It lasted from about 10,000 BC to around 2000 BC. People started using the Earth in a more sophisticated way. In the Stone Age, prehistoric people used stone tools which they made by chipping away at flint and other types of stone. In the New Stone Age, people created polished or shaped tools, such as the stone axe, to clear farmland and prepare it for crops, and to build more sophisticated homes.

SECRETS OF THE EARTH

You may be wondering how we know so much about the lives of our early ancestors? After all, human prehistory began around 3 million years ago, and there are no written records for us to study. So where have scientists found the evidence to support their ideas? As little as 250 years ago, few people were aware of prehistory, but the secrets of the past were about to be unearthed.

READING THE ROCKS

From the late 18th century to the mid 19th century, the Industrial Revolution took place (see pages 162-163). Great engines dug deep down into the Earth in search of coal. In developing industrial nations such as Britain and Germany, scientists began to learn how to read the rocks. They learnt that layers of rock were always found in the same order, and contained the same types of fossil. They realised that the Earth's history could be read from the sequence of fossils found in the layers of rocks.

ADDING UP THE BEGATS

Before we learnt to read the fossil record held in rocks, and before we began to understand our ancient history, many of our ancestors believed the Bible was a historically accurate record of ancient times. People relied on the stories in the Bible to explain how the world was created and where people came from. Many thought that the animals of the world came to exist because they survived on Noah's Ark during the time of the great flood. To work out the age of the Earth, scholars added up the 'begats'; the long list of births and deaths found in the stories at the beginning of the Old Testament in the Bible. Using this method, scholars reckoned that the beginning of time was around 4000 BC!

THE FOSSIL RECORD

Being able to read rocks and piece together the fossils contained inside them changed how people thought about the world. The fossil record revealed the remains of huge beasts that no longer stalked the Earth. The discovery of dinosaurs and other strange creatures led scientists to a startling conclusion: planet Earth must be truly ancient to account for all the changes found in the fossil record. They also realised that evidence of older humans must be visible somewhere in the structure of our planet. All they needed to do to learn more was dig!

FOSSIL READINGS

When scientists realised the story of Earth's history was in the ground, they started digging. What they found was truly remarkable. Imprints of jaw-dropping flowers that no-one had ever seen in bloom. Huge woolly mammoths that looked like elephants in need of a haircut. And of course enormous dinosaurs, along with a whole host of bizarre beasts that looked like they had all just walked out of a dream! The first scientist to study fossils was a Frenchman, Baron Georges Cuvier, in the 19th century. He is sometimes called the 'Father of **palaeontology**', after the new branch of science he invented.

AGE OF THE EARTH

Planet Earth is 4.54 billion years old. This date is based on dating samples from meteorites and Earth's rocks.

THEORY OF EVOLUTION

A scientist named Charles Darwin came to a startling conclusion about the secrets of the Earth: the theory of evolution. He and a few other scientists realised that extinct animals and plants found in Earth's rocks, together with the huge variety of living organisms, could only mean one thing: that populations of living things had changed over time. The theory of evolution also says that all living things are related. If you go back far enough in time, all animals, plants and living things had one ancestor – a single-celled organism similar to a bacterium. One **species** evolved into many millions, over millions of years.

CLOCKS IN THE ROCKS

Evolution needs millions and millions of years for changes on and in the planet to happen. To understand the age of the planet, scientists had to figure out a way to date the rocks. Luckily there are clocks in the rocks! Buried deep inside rocks are many chemical elements, and some of these elements are radioactive, which means they change from one type of chemical into another. The amount of time it takes for exactly half of one chemical element to change into another is known as the 'half-life'. We can measure the percentage of change that has happened and, using the half-life time, work out how long an element has been in the rock.

URANIUM HALF-LIFE

We know that the half-life of uranium-238 is roughly 4.47 billion years, and uranium-235 is 704 million years, which makes the element of uranium very useful when we are trying to date the age of the Earth.

DIGGING FOR TREASURE

Fossils are relics of our prehistoric past and they are found all over the Earth. When we talk about fossils, most people think about plant and animal remains preserved in rock. But tools and **artefacts** from human history and culture can also be fossilised over time. Sometimes fossils take the form of imprints left in rock. The imprints may be made by bones, feathers, human or animal footprints, and even dung!

HOW TO MAKE A FOSSIL

1. An animal or object falls on sand, or soft mud, and is quickly covered by sediment from ash or a landslide.

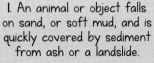

2. If an animal falls in a lake or a river and isn't moved, water drops sediments on top without disturbing the animal.

3. Over many years, layer upon layer of sediment covers the animal. Moisture is squeezed out and a chemical process turns the animal into a fossil in the layer of rock.

4. Movements of plates on the Earth's surface push the fossil up towards the surface and rock **erosion** or landslides mean that the fossil is near the surface or uncovered.

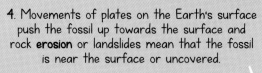

FOOTPRINTS IN THE MUD

About 20,000 years ago, five prehistoric hunters sprinted across the soft clay on the edge of a wetland in what is now Mungo National Park in Australia. Over time, the mud around their footprints hardened and turned to rock, fossilising their footprints. The prints were found next to a set of small, round holes, where a man probably stood with a spear. And a squiggle in the mud may have been a drawing done by a child.

5. Look for sedimentary rocks (see page 19), as they're the most common type of rock to hold fossils.

4. Organise a dig where you know fossils may be found – if there's one, there's bound to be more to find!

FIND A FOSSIL

Fossils lie like hidden secrets in many places around the Earth. Here are some tips to give yourself the best chance of finding one, like the fossilised imprint of a snail shown here.

3. Look along riverbanks as flowing water cuts deep into rock layers over the years, and that often exposes fossils.

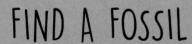

2. Look for an area where there has been a landslide as this turns the land upside down and may have thrown up a fossil or two. Don't go if it has happened recently though, as the area will be dangerous.

1. Professional fossil hunters can buy all sorts of hi-tech stuff, but finding fossils will always come down to the most essential tool – your eyes!

HUMANS AND THE EARTH

You and everyone else on the planet are all members of one family – and it is a big one! There are seven and a half billion people on Earth. We speak over 6,000 different languages in almost 200 countries. We come in all colours, shapes and sizes – just take a walk down a street in any big city and you will see this amazing **diversity** for yourself. How can we explain all this variety? What happened in our history to explain how different you are to almost everyone else? And where did your ancient ancestors (your great, great, x 2,000 grandparents!) live on the planet? Read on to find out...

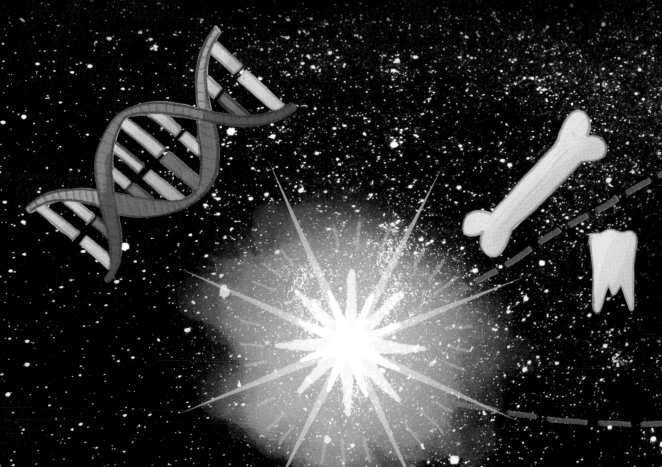

There is calcium in your teeth and bones, as well as in rocks such as chalk, limestone and marble.

MADE OF THE SAME STUFF AS STARS!

Believe it or not, the ingredients that make up your body are the same as those inside stars and planets. Under your skin you'll find blood, bones, muscles and organs. These are all made of the same chemical elements as the Earth, Moon and stars.

THINGS WE HAVE IN COMMON

This section of the book looks at the human journey across the planet and explains how we discovered that we are all members of one big family. It's important to realise that all people have more in common than not, even though we look and seem so different. We originally came from the same place on Earth, and we are all made of the same stuff, so we must be very alike.!

Other chemicals 3.7%

Nitrogen 3.3%

Hydrogen 9.5%

Carbon 18.5%

Oxygen 65%

The element iron, which is found in many places on the planet, is also found in your blood.

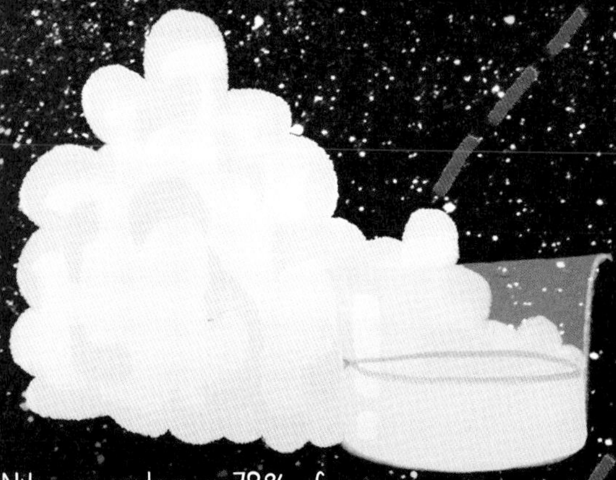

Nitrogen makes up 78% of our planet's atmosphere, and it's a vital ingredient in the important chemical **DNA** found inside our bodies.

Diamonds are made of pure carbon, which is also found in your skin.

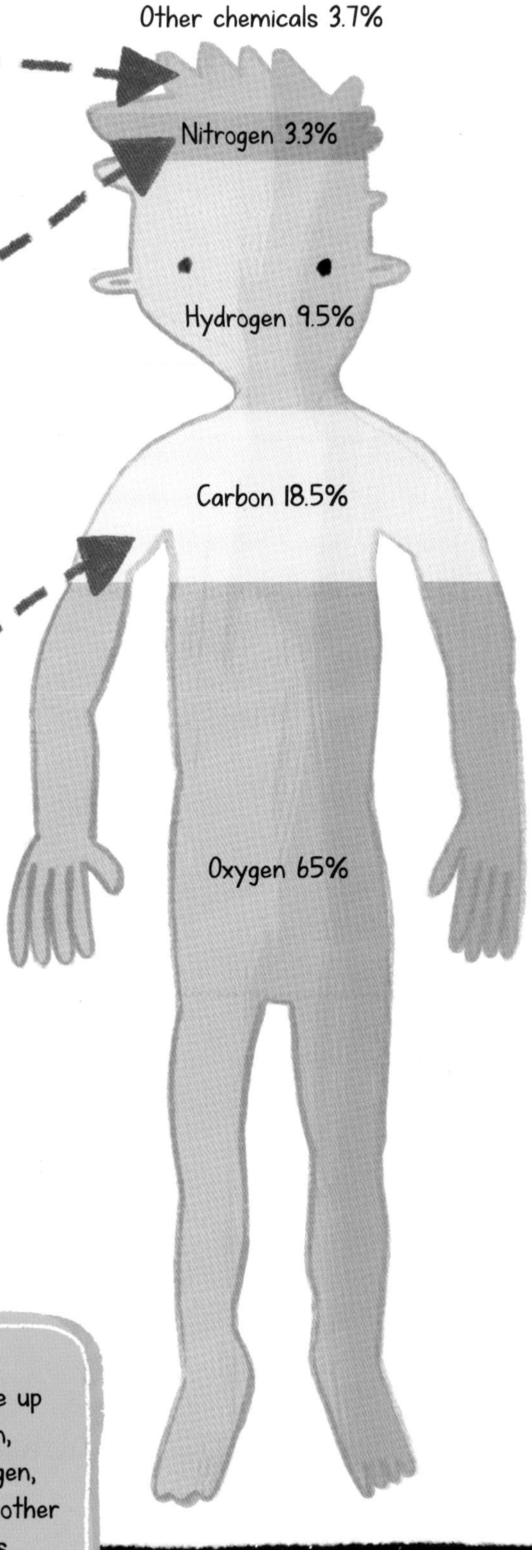

Our bodies are made up of oxygen, carbon, hydrogen and nitrogen, plus tiny amounts of other chemical elements.

DNA: THE CODE OF LIFE

Stand in front of a mirror... you're looking at a body that is made up of trillions of **cells**, the basic unit of all living things! There are many different kinds of cells, and each type does a different job, but the inside of almost every cell is the same. Most cells have a centre, called a nucleus, which carries 99.9% of your **genes**. Genes carry important information about who you are. In total your body has around 20,000 genes.

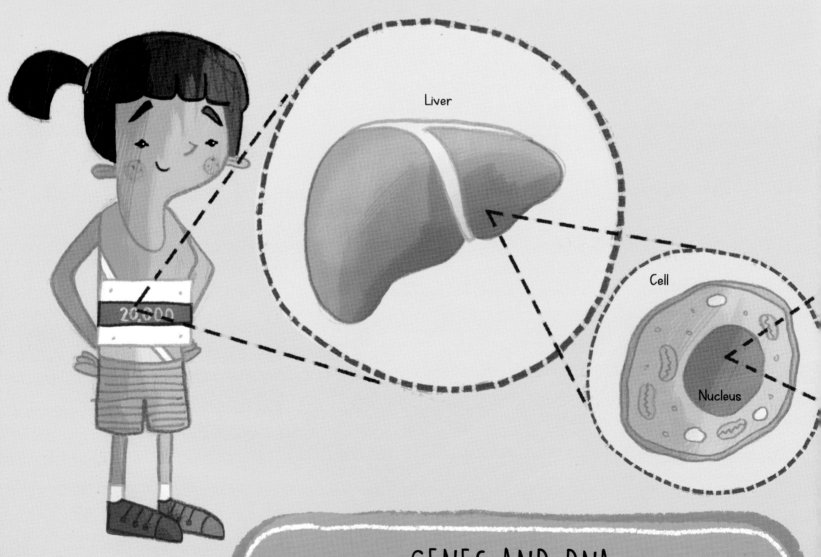

Liver

20,000

Cell

Nucleus

GENES AND DNA

Your genes are small parts of a chemical called DNA. There is nearly 2 m (6.5 ft) of DNA squeezed into almost every tiny human cell, but it is scrunched up so tightly that it is squeezed inside the nucleus. The information in genes is stored in a section called a 'base'. There are four types of base and the number and order of the bases in each gene section decides, for example, whether you are a banana, a chimpanzee, a cow or a human being. Think of genes as recipes – the combination of bases are the ingredients that change the end result. These recipes are passed from generation to generation!

IT'S IN YOUR GENES

You may have heard someone say, 'you have your mother's eyes' but what does that mean? Scientifically it means, 'you appear to have inherited genes from your mother which make a protein that tells your cells to make eyes that look like your mother's'! Genes tell a cell how to work, and what to look like or how to behave.

THE CHEMICALS IN DNA

DNA is a chemical made of sugar, phosphate and four different bases called A, T, C and G for short. These are all chemicals, too.

DNA LADDER

Imagine DNA is a coiled chemical ladder. If you string out the DNA from every cell in your body, end to end, it would reach from here to the Moon and back 3,000 times!

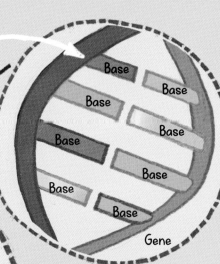

Base
Base
Base
Base
Base
Base
Base
Gene

DNA

Chromosome

CHROMOSOME COUNT!

DNA is organised into chunks called **chromosomes** which appear together in pairs. Different species have different numbers of chromosomes. Humans beings have 46 chromosomes, or 23 pairs. Chimpanzees have 24 pairs, chickens have 39 pairs, fruit flies have 4 pairs and bananas have 11 pairs of chromosomes.

THE DNA FAMILY

DNA shows how all life on Earth is related. You share 98.8% of your DNA with chimpanzees, and almost 90% with mice! And you share roughly 60% with chickens! But with other people, we share 99.8% of our DNA. So why do people seem so different? Turn the page to learn about the Gene Trail!

THE GENE TRAIL

The information in our genes is passed on from **generation** to generation when humans reproduce and a baby is born. On page 52 we talked about how the bases in DNA are like ingredients in a recipe that make a gene. And lots of genes make up the complete meal of DNA! Human bodies are clever and make new cells containing DNA all the time. Generally they just make copies of existing cells and follow the recipe to create the same DNA meal. Sometimes, however, a mistake happens and the cell copy isn't exactly identical, like varying the amount of one ingredient in a recipe. We call these small changes 'mutations', and we all have them. When parents pass their small mutations on to their children, this changed part of the recipe is called a 'marker'.

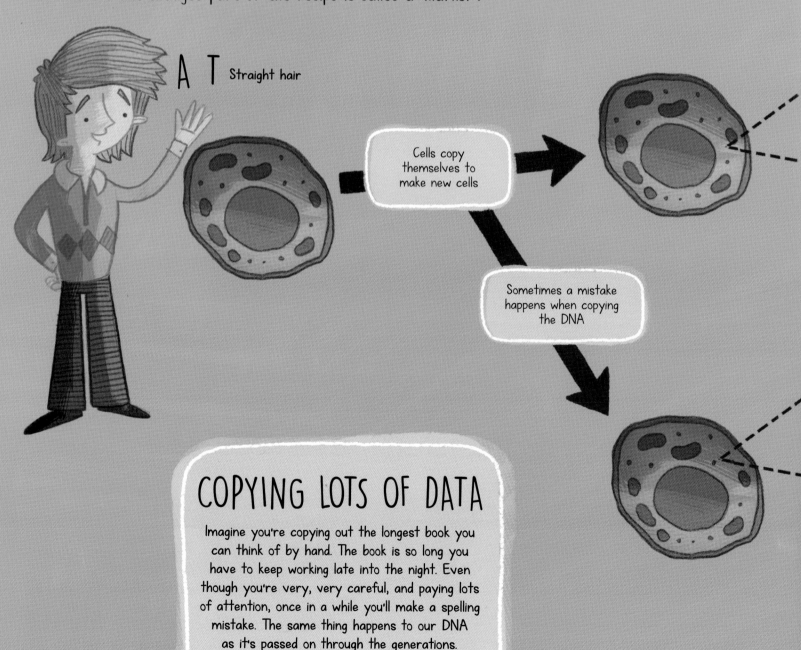

A T Straight hair

Cells copy themselves to make new cells

Sometimes a mistake happens when copying the DNA

COPYING LOTS OF DATA

Imagine you're copying out the longest book you can think of by hand. The book is so long you have to keep working late into the night. Even though you're very, very careful, and paying lots of attention, once in a while you'll make a spelling mistake. The same thing happens to our DNA as it's passed on through the generations. That's how markers occur.

YOU AND YOUR NEIGHBOUR!

Since markers are passed down from generation to generation, the number of differences between your DNA and your neighbour's will show how closely related you are. There are about 10 million markers in humans and these markers account for many of the genetic differences between you and everyone else on the planet.

PHENOTYPES

Your observable human traits (such as height and hair colour) are also known as your phenotype.

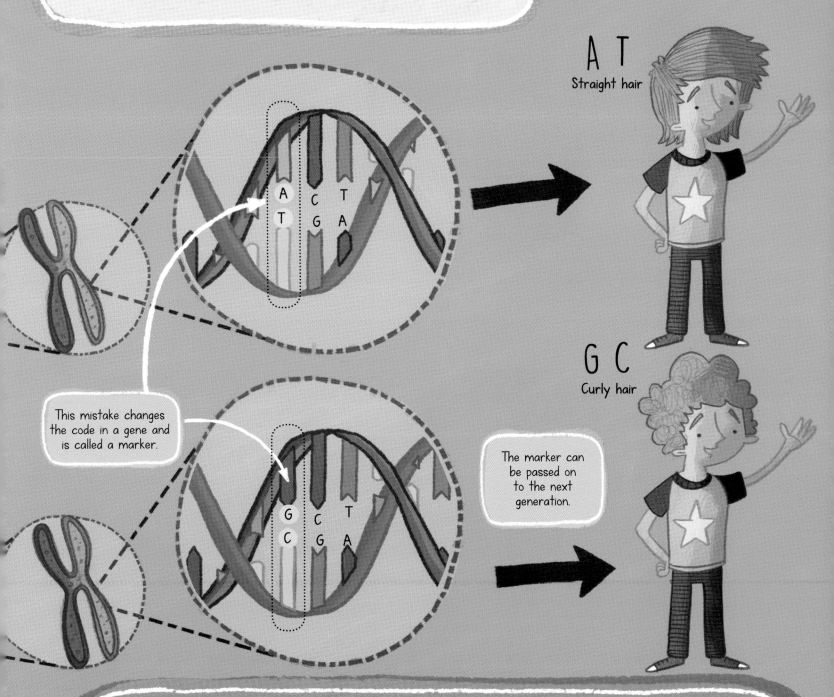

A T
Straight hair

G C
Curly hair

This mistake changes the code in a gene and is called a marker.

The marker can be passed on to the next generation.

IT'S IN YOUR BLOOD!

Markers in genes can be used as a type of time machine. We can take a look back into Earth's history using human blood! Inside every drop of blood is the best history book ever written and you are carrying a unique chapter in your veins. Scientists have taken blood samples from people all around the planet, looked at the markers and found some quite incredible things. All humans alive today come from the same big family tree. Around 200,000 years ago, there were only about 2,000 humans, living in Africa. A small group left on a long journey and you are one of their children. Read on to find out more!

OUT OF AFRICA

The first stop on our human journey is Africa – the birthplace of our human ancestors. A particular DNA marker can be traced back, through the blood of different peoples, to the first time and place where that marker was created – in Africa. For many thousands of years, Homo sapiens lived throughout the African continent but only some of these people are our ancestors. About 60,000 years ago, a group of them began their journey out of Africa. As our ancestors moved to new places and **habitats**, they became isolated from other groups. This is how differences, or the high level of human diversity, began.

WHY LEAVE AFRICA?

Why did our early ancestors leave their home? One clue is that there's very little **archaeological** evidence in parts of Africa between 60,000 and 30,000 years ago. Temperatures had dropped, the seas had retreated and Africa was drying up. Scientists believe there was an Ice Age between 70,000 and 50,000 years ago, which means that more of the Earth's water had become locked up in ice, and the non-ice parts of Earth were really dry.

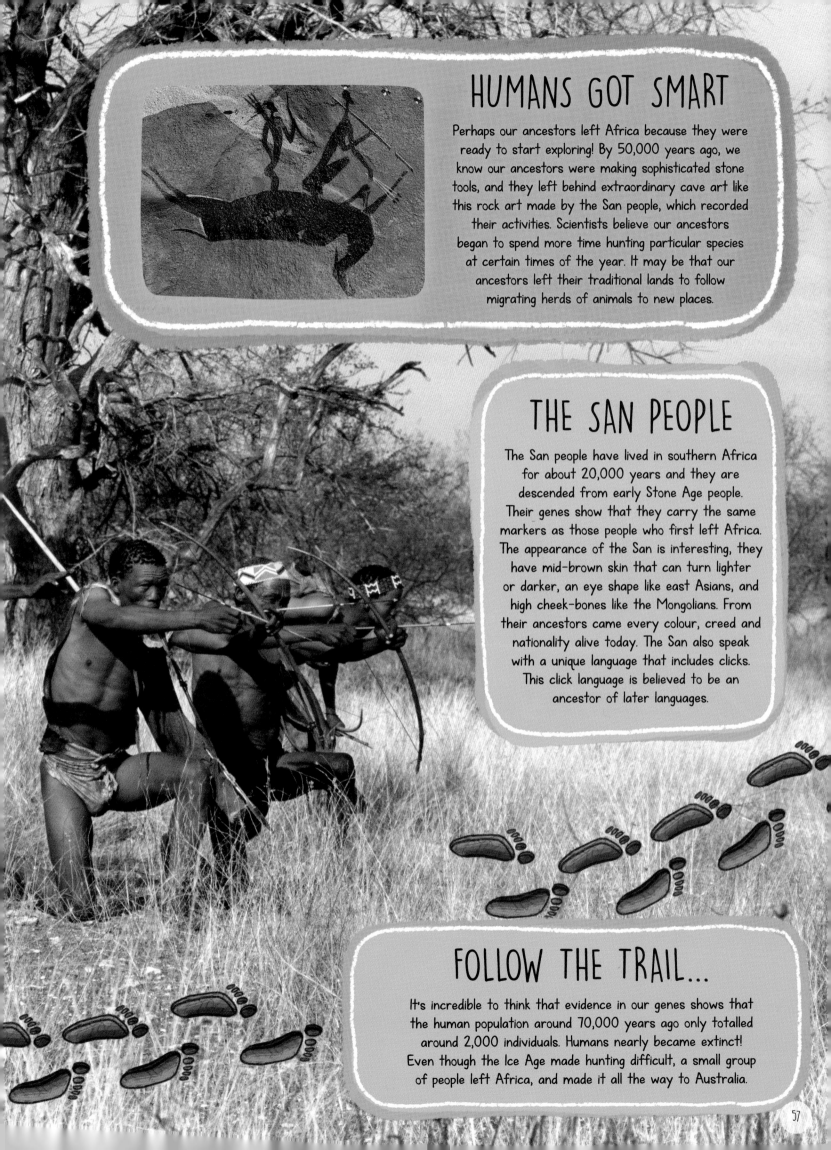

HUMANS GOT SMART

Perhaps our ancestors left Africa because they were ready to start exploring! By 50,000 years ago, we know our ancestors were making sophisticated stone tools, and they left behind extraordinary cave art like this rock art made by the San people, which recorded their activities. Scientists believe our ancestors began to spend more time hunting particular species at certain times of the year. It may be that our ancestors left their traditional lands to follow migrating herds of animals to new places.

THE SAN PEOPLE

The San people have lived in southern Africa for about 20,000 years and they are descended from early Stone Age people. Their genes show that they carry the same markers as those people who first left Africa. The appearance of the San is interesting, they have mid-brown skin that can turn lighter or darker, an eye shape like east Asians, and high cheek-bones like the Mongolians. From their ancestors came every colour, creed and nationality alive today. The San also speak with a unique language that includes clicks. This click language is believed to be an ancestor of later languages.

FOLLOW THE TRAIL...

It's incredible to think that evidence in our genes shows that the human population around 70,000 years ago only totalled around 2,000 individuals. Humans nearly became extinct! Even though the Ice Age made hunting difficult, a small group of people left Africa, and made it all the way to Australia.

AUSTRALIA

How do we know early humans travelled to Australia? And how did they get there, when there is so little archaeological evidence of their journey? The answer to the first question is easy enough: we know Australia separated from Pangea around 100 million years ago and there were no **native** animals on the land mass from which humans could have evolved. This means humans must have come to Australia from somewhere else – they must have travelled there from their origins in Africa!

HOW MANY HUMANS TRAVELLED?

Scientists estimate that from a population of 2,000 to 5,000 individuals in Africa, only a small group, possibly as few as 150 people, crossed the Red Sea. Though the Sea never completely froze over during the Ice Age, it was narrow enough and there may have been islands to enable careful crossing using rafts.

ALL TO THEMSELVES

Think about the small band of humans who landed in northern Australia, arriving on a primitive raft. They must have planned it, making sure there were enough men and women to set up a new population there. Guided by rivers, they ventured inland, where they found new creatures, but no other humans. This intrepid group had a new continent all to themselves!

THE PATH OF THEIR JOURNEY

The first travellers journeyed eastward out of Africa. The most obvious journey was along the coast of southern Asia, as the coastal route has no big change in climate or environment. Our intrepid travellers, and their descendants, took this beachcombing coastal route, reaching present-day Malaysia within a few thousand years. But how did they cross the 90 km (56 mi) of ocean, which separates Australia from Indonesia? Remember: 50,000 years ago there was still an ice age! Some of the world's water was locked up in ice so sea levels were lower, and Indonesia was one land mass. Only one small sea-crossing was needed to reach Australia.

EVIDENCE IN THE ROCKS

By 45,000 years ago, humans were settled in parts of Australia. We know this because there's archaeological evidence that Aboriginal Australians have been on the continent for that long. They made campfires, which can still be detected, and they left their mark in cave art.

INDIA ⫸ ASIA

Australia was the first route out of Africa. The descendants of the second route would become Asians, Europeans and Native Americans. In other words, everyone else on the planet! Scientists believe they've spotted the same marker in the genes of Chinese, Russians, Native Americans, Europeans and most Indians. Incredibly, all those peoples share a marker inherited from a single male human in the distant past. He was in the second band of travellers to strike out of Africa, and they took an alternative route - to the Middle East.

Vesuvius

THROUGH THE MIDDLE EAST

Around 45,000 years ago the Earth was already cold because an ice age had started 70,000 years ago. But then, it got even colder. It is thought that the average temperature dropped 20°C (68°F) in some places. The grassy plains of Africa would have shrunk back. Small bands of humans would have gone hungry for hundreds, if not thousands, of years. Drought would have made animals, and their human predators, move out of places like the Sahara in Africa, looking for new lands. They travelled through the Middle East to get from Africa to the rest of the world.

TO PLACES BEYOND

This second small group of humans set out on a trek inland, through the Middle East and into southern Central Asia. From there, our ancestors made later journeys to destinations in Asia, Europe and beyond. One band made a journey into India. This tiny group did so well that their numbers swelled, almost drowning all traces of the earlier coastal migration to Australia. A second band journeyed to China. This part of the world is surrounded by mountains and sea, making it hard to reach, so this group of people were isolated. Their isolation meant they developed a distinctive look.

TWO WAVES INTO ASIA

Scientists believe that genetic markers show Asia was settled in two waves of migration. One wave was to the north. The other wave was to the south of the mountain ranges. Humans got to India and China (and Australia!) before they got to Europe.

To the Philippines

Toba

Tambora

To Australia

SUPER-VOLCANO

There's also a super-volcano theory behind why humans started travelling out of Africa. The super-volcano in question is called Toba, and it's in Indonesia. Around 70,000 years ago, Toba suffered a gargantuan explosion. If you thought Vesuvius and Tambora from page 31 were deadly, Toba was thousands of times more powerful. It dumped 6 cm (2.4 in) of ash – a layer that can still be seen in the fossil record – on all lands of South Asia, the Indian Ocean, the Arabian and South China Seas. With so much ash and dust in the air, the Sun was dimmed for years. The land would have become like a giant ashtray, with ash clogging rivers and streams, and seasonal rains stopping. Is this why humans were forced to keep moving around the globe looking for better land?

TOBA

TAMBORA

VESUVIUS

EUROPE

The next stop on our journey is Europe. Humans first got to Europe around 45,000 years ago. Europe was a cold and icy place, so to help them survive their skin got paler over many generations to help them absorb more light and make vitamin D. Coastal peoples to the south of Europe stayed a little darker skinned, as they got their vitamin D by eating seafood so didn't need help from sunlight. The Ice Age cut off this European group of travellers from their ancestors in Africa so they had no contact with the rest of the world for thousands of years. In isolation, Europeans grew taller and developed a distinctive nose shape.

WINTER HUNTERS

The first group of soon-to-be Europeans followed the hunt. They tracked animals and food, developing their hunting skills as they went. When humans moved into Europe they faced harsh challenges as it was much colder here. They also had to cope with Neanderthals. The Neanderthals had been living in Europe for hundreds of thousands of years and they were better suited to the cold climate as they had stocky, robust figures with more hair. But Homo sapiens were very skilled with tools and could make warm clothes. The two different human populations shared Europe, for around 5,000 years, before Neanderthals finally met their downfall.

THREE WAVES

Recent thinking suggests there may have actually been three waves of people migrating to Europe. The appearance of modern native peoples in Europe is influenced by these three separate waves of humans.

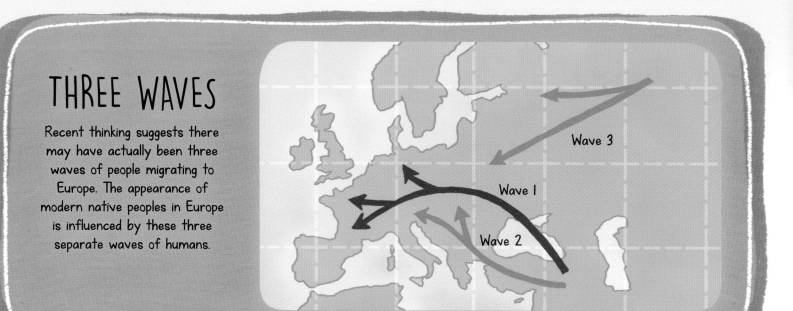

WAVE 1

Wave one was the hunter-gatherer people of 45,000 years ago. They most likely came from Africa into Europe and had dark skin as they got their vitamin D from the animals they ate rather than sunlight. It is thought they may also have brought the blue eye gene with them, which is common in modern European humans today.

WAVE 2

Wave two were early farmers who journeyed into Europe about 9,000 years ago and mixed in with the hunter-gatherers already living there. They tended to have paler skin so they could absorb more light and make vitamin D as they got less of it from their food.

WAVE 3

Wave three came from Central Asia around 5,000 years ago. These people were the first to domesticate horses, and they've contributed their DNA to a wide range of modern humans, including Native Americans.

SWEEPING GRASSLANDS

When our ancestors reached Eurasia, they found a grassland super-highway. The grasslands during the Ice Age stretched from Europe all the way over to what we now call Korea, in northeast Asia. The entire land mass was open to roaming.

THE AMERICAS

The final chapter of our Earth story takes us to the Americas. This leg of the journey started in Asia, and ended up in north and south America. Boffins believe the ancestors of the Americans crossed from Siberia in Russia into Alaska. But how did they do that when today, for about six months during the long winter, the Bering Sea between the two land masses is clogged solid with ice? Not even modern ice-breaker boats can get through, so how did our human ancestors manage it over 20,000 years ago?

BERINGIA

The answer once again is to be found in the Ice Age. As sea levels dropped, a new land mass, now named Beringia, rose up from beneath the Bering Sea. This new land provided a path from the Russian east coast to Alaska. It's likely that animals headed for new pastures, and their human hunters simply followed them into new territory, and into this new continent.

A NEW WORLD

Once the ice began to thaw, the explorers appear to have trekked down from Alaska, through a corridor east of the Rocky Mountains. As ice gave way to rolling prairies, they found before them a 'new world' – an uninhabited continent with lots of roaming bison and mammoths. The journey that had begun in Africa, and divided in Asia, had now reached the last corner of the Earth, the last continent. The ancestors of this group of humans had found a new home. Together they'd survived drought, famine and an ice age to get there!

Russia

Bering Sea

Alaska

SOME BOFFINS BELIEVE THAT THE FIRST GROUP TO REACH ALASKA MAY HAVE BEEN ONLY 10 OR 20 PEOPLE. BUT WITHIN 1,000 YEARS THERE WERE PEOPLE LIVING IN BOTH NORTH AND SOUTH AMERICA.

NORTH AMERICA
THE NAVAJO

A Native American tribe called the Navajo (see page 184) has a gene marker inherited from the Chukchi, a tribe who still lives deep in Arctic Russia. It is thought the Chukchi were a group who stayed put in Russia on the trail from Asia to America, while others carried on their journey and became the Navajo people in North America.

SOUTH AMERICA
THE ANDEANS

South America's oldest-known human occupation site is the 14,600-year-old Monte Verde settlement in the Andes. The skeletons found in the mountains suggests that humans got there quickly after crossing into the continent across the Bering land bridge, one or two thousand years earlier. The Andeans living here developed a resistance to altitude sickness.

THE WORLD TODAY

Humans are of the Earth. We evolved from the Earth and our bodies are made up of the same chemical elements that are found in the depths of the Earth. Once evolution was well underway, our ancestors emerged in Africa. A small group of Africans decided to set out on an incredible journey, and from there it took us only 35,000 years to make the journey by foot from Africa all the way to the Americas. This Earth story is partly carried in the blood of everyone reading this book. We are one big family, separated by only 2,000 generations!

WHY WE LOOK THE WAY WE DO

The way modern humans look is down to two main influences. The first influence is from Africa and is shared by all living humans – a high and rounded skull, a small brow and a bony chin. These traits evolved in Africa around 100,000 years ago and were carried by our ancestors on the journey that began about 60,000 years ago. The second influence on how we look today is what gave us different features in different geographic regions. These are the differently shaped faces and eyelids and different hair and skin colours that distinguish human populations. The way modern humans evolved was shaped by the places they moved to and lived in.

PATCHWORK PLANET

Scientists have recently discovered a twist in the tale of our story. Over 90% of our genes come from our common African heritage. But minor amounts of human DNA come from different origins. It seems the ancient journeys of humans out of Africa brought us into contact with different species. So humans met and bred with Neanderthals in Europe, and another species called the Denisovans in Australia, for example. Some races of humans have about 2.5% of their DNA from Neanderthals. Indigenous people living in Australia and New Guinea today have about 5% Denisovan DNA.

WHO ARE DENISOVANS?

Denisovans are an extinct ancient species of human. They are named after the discovery in 2010 of a finger bone fragment of a young female, who lived about 41,000 years ago. The bone was found in the remote Denisova Cave in Siberia.

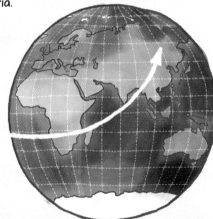

SCIENCE TODAY

This story of humans' link to Earth could only have been told today. Only recently have scientists learnt how to read the clues in our blood, our DNA and the elements that link us to the Earth. We are able to excavate Earth's past from the blood of people living in the present! The years to come may bring even more exciting discoveries.

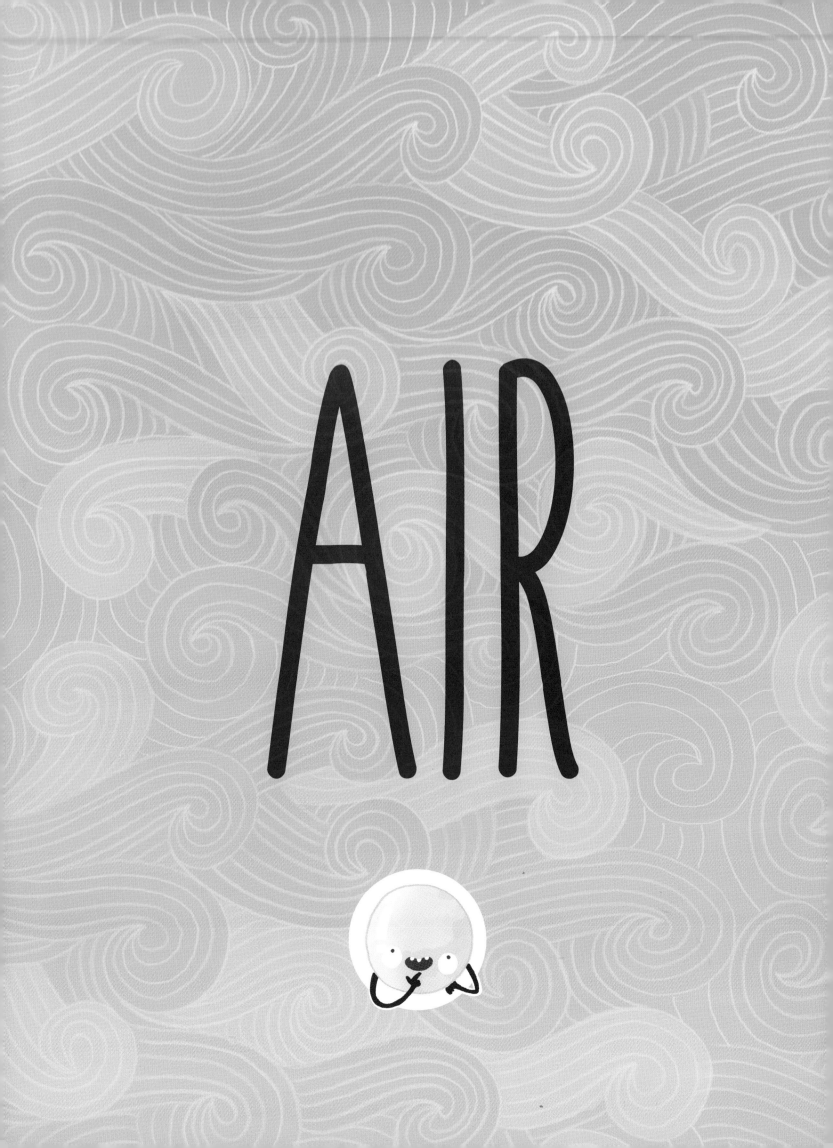

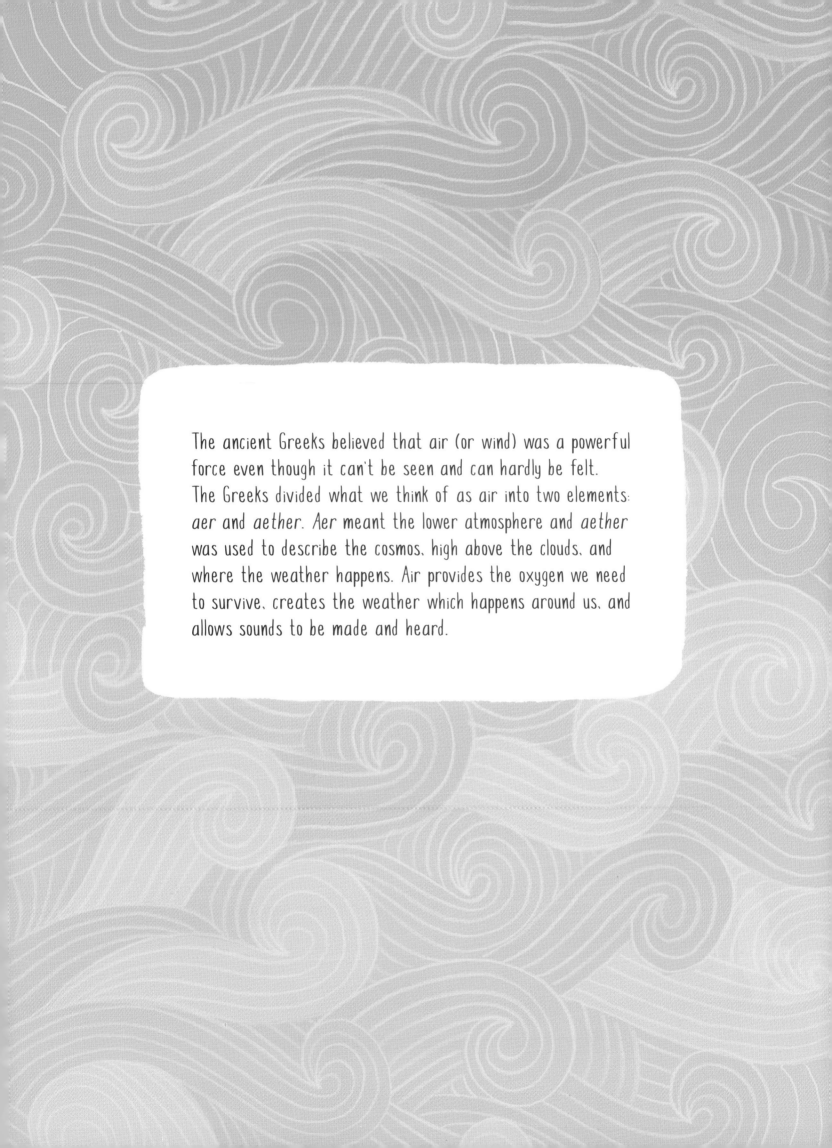

The ancient Greeks believed that air (or wind) was a powerful force even though it can't be seen and can hardly be felt. The Greeks divided what we think of as air into two elements: *aer* and *aether*. Aer meant the lower atmosphere and *aether* was used to describe the cosmos, high above the clouds, and where the weather happens. Air provides the oxygen we need to survive, creates the weather which happens around us, and allows sounds to be made and heard.

WHAT'S AIR MADE OF?

Take a deep breath. Do you know what you are breathing into your lungs? Air, of course! But what do we mean by that? Air is a mixture of invisible gases. Most of the gas is nitrogen, 78% in fact. Oxygen is another gas which makes up about 21% of air. Oxygen is important for human beings as our bodies use it to release energy from chemicals. Air also contains tiny amounts of other gases including argon, carbon dioxide and helium.

GASES IN THE AIR WE BREATHE

78% Nitrogen

AIR IS INVISIBLE

How do we know air is there if we can't see it? Try this simple experiment – blow against the palm of your hand. Can you feel your breath? This breath is air exhaled from your lungs. When you breathe out you are moving the air out of your lungs and blowing it onto your hand. Similarly, when the wind blows, it moves the air around us. We know it's there because we can feel it on our skin and see it move the trees around us.

WHO HAS SEEN THE WIND?

Think of air as molecules flowing like water. Air is fluid, even though it is a gas rather than a liquid. When air flows quickly from one place to another it creates wind. The wind is invisible but the effects of wind, from a gentle breeze to a violent hurricane, are very visible indeed! The creation of wind (flowing air) starts with the Sun. It heats the air, and when one area warms up more than another, there is a difference in pressure. These different air pockets of pressure push each other around from place to place, creating wind.

21% Oxygen

0.9% Argon

0.1% Other gases:
carbon dioxide,
xenon, neon,
hydrogen, helium,
kzrypton

SOLIDS, LIQUIDS AND GASES

All matter is made from solids, liquids or gases.

  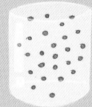

Solid things, such as wood, plastic or rock, hold their shape when poked or pushed. Their particles are packed tightly together and cannot move apart.

Liquid things, such as water, flow easily and change their shape. Their particles can move around each other but they still stay close together.

Gases, such as the air we breathe, have particles that float about freely as they are not connected to each other. Air fills the space it is in.

WATER IN THE AIR

When we talk about the composition of air, we usually mean the gases that make up the Earth's atmosphere. And yet the atmosphere also contains an amazing amount of water vapour, which is water in the form of a gas. In fact, there's enough water in the air to cover the entire surface of the world (land and sea) with 2.5 cm (1 in) of rain. When we talk about cloud, climate, weather and wind later in this chapter, remember it's the combination of water and air that makes these things all possible.

LAYERS OF AIR

The atmosphere is a fundamental part of planet Earth. It first formed, with the rest of our planet, more than 4.5 billion years ago (see pages 10-11 for more about this). Scientists divide the atmosphere into five layers, based on the different temperatures.

BALLOON MEASUREMENTS

To measure the conditions at different heights above the Earth's surface, scientists send up weather balloons. These balloons carry equipment that measures wind speed, temperature, pressure and humidity (the amount of water vapour in the air).

3. MESOSPHERE

The third layer of atmosphere is where the air really starts to get cold. Reaching out to 85 km (53 mi) above the Earth's surface, temperatures in the mesosphere dip as low as -130°C (-202°F). This is the layer of the atmosphere where small lumps of rock orbiting the Sun, called meteoroids, appear. As it enters the Earth's upper atmosphere, a meteoroid heats up and glows brightly, appearing as a meteor, or shooting star.

2. STRATOSPHERE

The stratosphere stretches above the troposphere to 50 km (31 mi) above Earth's surface. Imagine you can fly through the air, like a superhero. As you soar up through the troposphere it will gradually become cooler. But that will change when you reach the stratosphere. For the first 20 km (12.5 mi) of the stratosphere, the temperature will increase again, due to the presence of ozone gas. This gas absorbs lots of the Sun's radiation and heats the other air particles around it.

1. TROPOSPHERE

The troposphere begins at Earth's surface and reaches up 14 km (9 mi) high. This part of the atmosphere is the most dense as 80% of the air in the entire atmosphere sits here. The closer to Earth the air is, the more it is pulled down by gravity, and so the particles of air become more tightly packed together. Almost all weather happens in the troposphere and aircraft fly within it.

Space

Exosphere

Thermosphere

4. THERMOSPHERE

The fourth layer of air is known as the thermosphere and reaches up to 600 km (372 mi) high. Temperatures here can hit 1,700°C (3,090°F)! There are very few particles of air at this height but those that are here are super-heated by the Sun's light, which they absorb very quickly. There isn't any water vapour or clouds in the thermosphere. Sometimes, the Northern and Southern Lights can be seen in this layer (see pages 78–79).

5. EXOSPHERE

The outermost layer of the Earth's atmosphere is the exosphere. This layer of air is where our planet meets space. It reaches out to 10,000 km (6,200 mi). Past this point molecules of air no longer feel the pull of Earth's gravity. The bottom of the exosphere is where you'll find most of the satellites orbiting Earth.

Mesosphere

Stratosphere

Ozone layer

Troposphere

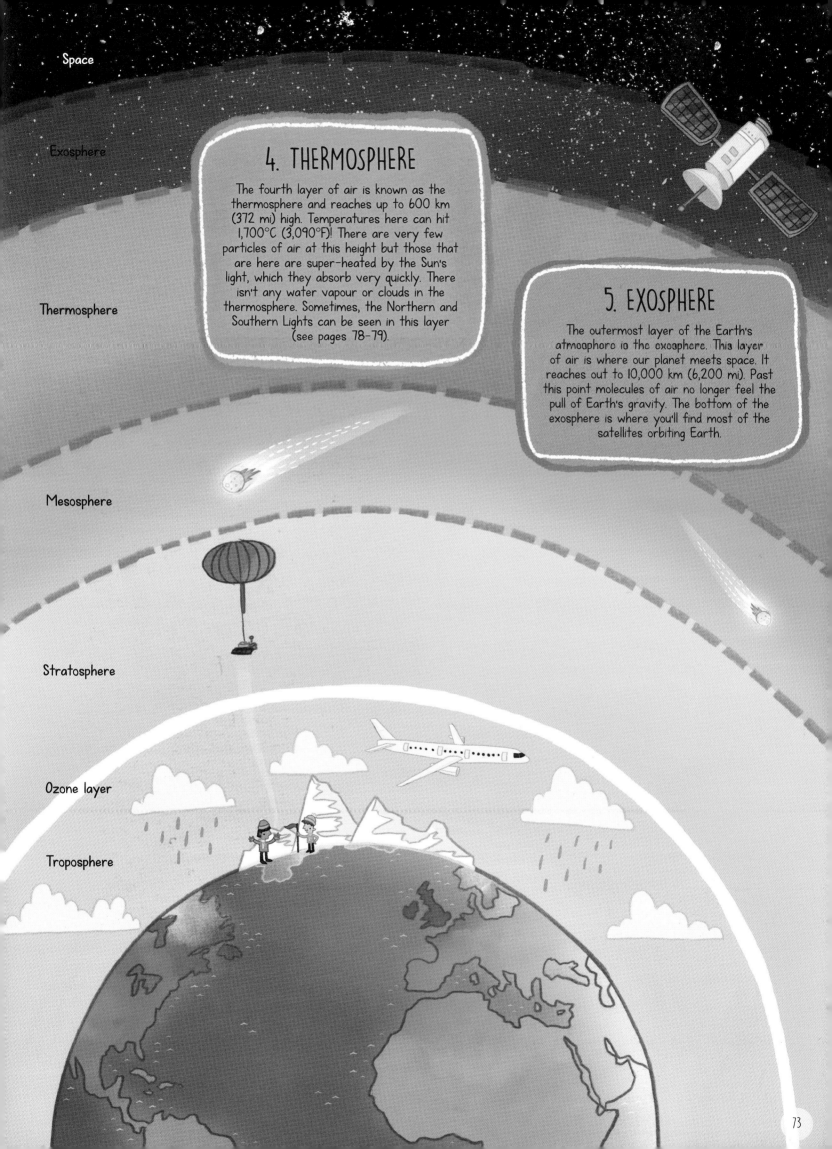

HOW AIR EVOLVED

The air is part of planet Earth, just like the land and sea. But the air on Earth today is not the same as it was over 4 billion years ago when our planet was very young. Air has evolved. It has changed from the thick, hazy air of the prehistoric past, to the mostly clear blue skies we see today. This is because the gases in air have changed over time. When living things appeared on Earth, they changed the composition of air by breathing in and out different amounts of the gases.

AIR BEFORE LIFE EXISTED

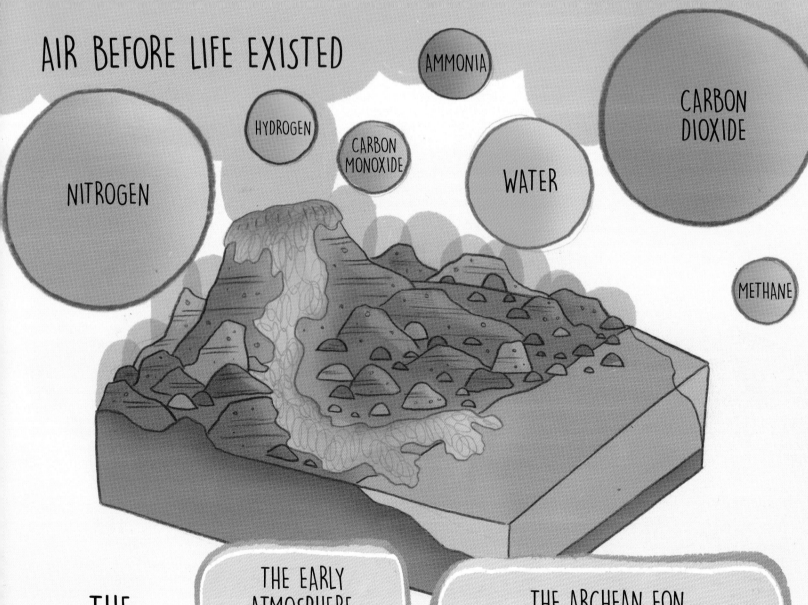

AMMONIA

HYDROGEN

CARBON MONOXIDE

NITROGEN

WATER

CARBON DIOXIDE

METHANE

THE EVOLUTION OF AIR

THE EARLY ATMOSPHERE
(4.5 bya)

As Earth cooled, the air around it was made up of gases that poured out of active volcanoes. These gases included methane, nitrogen, and far more carbon dioxide than today's atmosphere.

THE ARCHEAN EON
(4 to 2.5 bya)

The Earth was shrouded in a haze of methane gas at this time. There was no oxygen in the air and the earliest, simple forms of life did not need oxygen to survive. Then, 2.7 billion years ago, tiny blue-green organisms called cyanobacteria flourished in the seas (see pages 196-197). They made oxygen using carbon dioxide, water and sunlight in the process called photosynthesis. Over time, oxygen levels increased to make up 1% of the air.

PHOTOSYNTHESIS

Photosynthesis is the way living things use energy from sunlight to make their own food (see page 159). The process also creates oxygen. The first time photosynthesis happened on Earth was a hugely important event as it meant oxygen existed in the air for creatures to use. Over millions of years, the composition of air changed and eventually became what we know today.

IF OXYGEN LEVELS ON EARTH WERE UNDER 15% WE WOULDN'T BE ABLE TO CREATE FIRE. IF LEVELS WERE OVER 25% ORGANIC MATTER WOULD FREELY BURN AND THERE WOULD BE WILDFIRE EVERYWHERE.

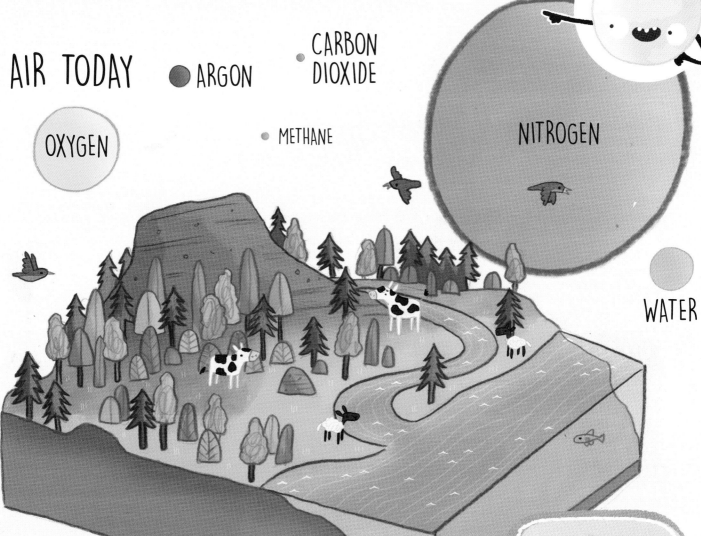

AIR TODAY

OXYGEN   ARGON   CARBON DIOXIDE

METHANE   NITROGEN   WATER

LIFE ON EARTH
(2.6 bya to 400 mya)

The air that we breathe and life on Earth evolved together. Over millions of years, tiny organisms made enough oxygen, which when combined with water, created a molecule that could break down methane gas in the atmosphere. This cleared the haze, and turned the sky blue.

THE OXYGEN BOOM
(700 to 550 mya)

The amount of oxygen in the sea and air increased dramatically. By 600 mya, oxygen levels in the air had reached 4%. The oxygen boom was vital for life forms that needed oxygen to create energy. For some other life forms, oxygen was poisonous. Those organisms became extinct.

AIR AS WE KNOW IT
(550 mya to today)

As the proportion of oxygen in the air increased (thanks to photosynthesis), levels of carbon dioxide decreased. Instead of being in the air, carbon became locked up in **fossil fuels**. The ocean and the carbon cycle maintained these levels (see pages 172–173). Today oxygen makes up 21% of air, and carbon dioxide is only 0.038%.

AIR GIVES LIFE

The increase in oxygen levels between 700 and 550 million years ago brought huge changes to life on Earth. Some organisms thrived, while other life forms died out. Scientists think that this oxygen boom helped fuel the surge in sea life, which appeared 530 to 509 million years ago.

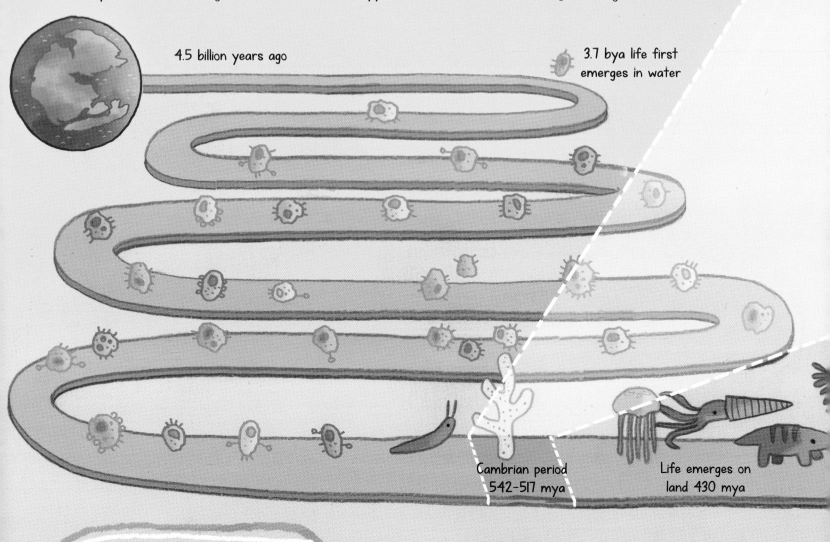

4.5 billion years ago

3.7 bya life first emerges in water

Cambrian period 542–517 mya

Life emerges on land 430 mya

OXYGEN LEGACY

You are an oxygen-loving organism. Your body uses oxygen to extract energy from food. You inherited this ability to use oxygen from ancient creatures that evolved using the oxygen in Earth's atmosphere. Without the life forms that went before, you wouldn't be here at all!

FROM SEA TO LAND

Before the Cambrian explosion, most life forms on Earth were simple, single-celled organisms, living on oxygen in seawater. Then, 430 mya, life began to emerge on land. Animals without backbones evolved the ability to absorb oxygen directly from the atmosphere.

THE CAMBRIAN EXPLOSION

The Cambrian explosion was an evolutionary period which started around 542 million years ago. During this time major animal features such as skeletons, hard shells, antennae, legs, joints and jaws evolved. This is shown in the fossil record (see pages 44-45). The 'explosion' lasted for around 25 million years. From then on, the diversity of life forms began to evolve into the plants and animals we know today.

Legs

Jaws

Shell

Antennae

Shell

Dinosaurs appear 230 mya

Dinosaurs became extinct 65 mya

Man evolves 200,000 ya

MODERN ATMOSPHERE

During most of the last 290 million years, the Earth was much warmer than it is now. The planet's polar ice caps were small or non-existent, and winters were warmer around the globe. Palm trees grew as far north as Canada, and many types of plants and animals lived in the Earth's polar areas. Scientists study the effects of gases in the air to understand the way in which our climate has changed. Read more about the climate on pages 110-111.

THE NORTHERN LIGHTS

The Northern Lights, or the aurora borealis, are one of nature's most wonderful sights. Between September and April, in countries in the Northern Hemisphere such as Norway, Iceland, Finland and Scotland, high above the **magnetic** pole, coloured lights skip and dance before your eyes. The patterns they make shift and change colour as you watch. Often, the lights resemble enormous bright curtains, hanging down from the sky. Then seconds later the lights change shape again.

AURORA BOREALIS

The source of the Northern Lights is even more incredible than their appearance. People may travel thousands of kilometres just to see the lights, but what creates the lights (also known as aurora borealis) has travelled much further. The Northern Lights are made by highly charged particles carried to Earth by solar winds. They travel all the way from the Sun, at speeds of up to 1.6 million km/h (1 million mph)!

MAGNETIC EFFECTS

Less than two days after leaving the Sun, the charged particles enter the Earth's atmosphere, creating a spectacular display of light. The particles in the solar winds strike the atmosphere anywhere from 80 to 800 km (50 to 500 mi) above the surface of the planet. They follow the lines of magnetic force made by the Earth's core and flow to an area of highly charged electrical and magnetic fields. The colour of the light they create depends on what gases they meet, and where they are in the atmosphere.

Aurora borealis above the North Pole

COLOUR–CODED SKY

The Northern and Southern Lights occur along 'ovals', which is what we see from below as those huge curtains of colour. There is a colour code behind the display:

  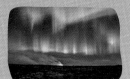 

GREEN	RED	BLUE	PURPLE/VIOLET
Particles meet oxygen, up to around 240 km (149 mi) above the planet.	Particles meet oxygen, more than 240 km (149 mi) above the planet.	Particles meet nitrogen, up to around 97 km (60 mi) above the planet.	Particles meet nitrogen, more than 97 km (60 mi) above the planet.

Aurora australis above the South Pole

AURORA AUSTRALIS

The particles carried by solar winds also reach the magnetic South Pole and create the same light shows in the Southern Hemisphere. There, they are called the Southern Lights, or aurora australis.

COMFORT IN THE COLOURS

The amazing light displays at the North and South Poles remind us that Earth's atmosphere protects us from solar and cosmic dangers on a daily basis. Even relatively large meteors, which would otherwise hurtle towards the ground, are burnt up high above our heads, in the thick protective layers of the atmosphere.

LEARNING TO FLY

Today, we take flight for granted. Insects buzz around our head, birds fly from tree to tree, and bats flit in the night sky. But how did early reptiles, bats and birds develop the ability to take to the sky millions of years ago, and more importantly, why?

EVOLUTION

The theory of evolution says that all living things are related. When mutations in genes happen (see pages 54-55), changes are passed from existing species to future generations, and organic life becomes more varied. On page 46, we discovered that scientists can read the fossil record and work out how living creatures have changed over the course of history. Scientists can examine the fossil record and find evidence of the first life forms that evolved for flight. This is a fossilised pterosaur, found in Germany.

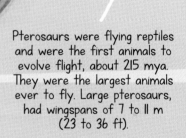

Pterosaurs were flying reptiles and were the first animals to evolve flight, about 215 mya. They were the largest animals ever to fly. Large pterosaurs, had wingspans of 7 to 11 m (23 to 36 ft).

QUETZALCOATLUS NORTHROPI WAS THE LARGEST OF ALL THE PTEROSAURS. IT WAS AS HEAVY AS A PIANO AND AS LONG AS A LONDON BUS!

HOW TO WING IT

The fossil record shows us that once certain creatures had evolved the basic ability to fly, their descendants adapted further and became even more efficent flyers. Flying animals had several advantages over land-based creatures. They could seek out new land, escape predators more quickly and hunt more effectively from the sky. And they could raise chicks in safe, hard-to-reach places, like this kittiwake. These were the animals with the highest chance of survival.

PTEROSAURS, BIRDS AND BATS

Three different animal groups developed the ability to fly: pterosaurs, birds and bats. Scientists study the fossil remains of each of these groups of animals, to work out how they evolved for flight. But there is still one unanswered question: Why did flight evolve at all? Scientists are not sure if flight evolved from the ground up (from a ground-running creature, for example), or from the treetops down (from a leaping or gliding ancestor).

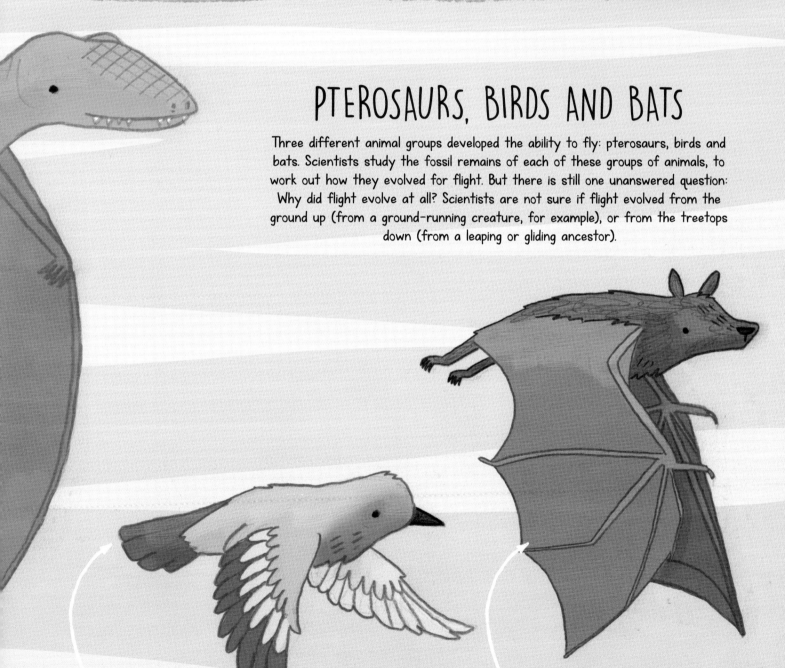

The earliest birds appeared 140 mya. Unlike the pterosaurs, birds descended from dinosaurs. Most importantly, they evolved feathers.

Bats evolved around 60 mya. They probably evolved from a gliding ancestor. Like the pterosaurs, their wings are a thin membrane of skin, stretched over a bony, hand-like frame.

DINOSAURS IN THE AIR?

Scientists who study dinosaurs are called palaentologists. They think that pterosaurs were among the first animals to fly, and that they evolved from a running creature about 225 million years ago. Most people think that pterosaurs were dinosaurs. They lived at the same time as dinosaurs, and became extinct around the same time, but in fact they were reptiles. Before they died out, around 66 million years ago, pterosaurs had evolved the ability to fly.

WHY DID PTEROSAURS FLY?

So why did pterosaurs begin to fly? Perhaps flight helped them escape from predators. Or, maybe it enabled them to catch quick-footed prey. Either way, flight would definitely have been an advantage because creatures that can leap or glide through the air are harder to catch! Being able to fly meant the pterosaurs could find new places to hunt and found prey easier to catch.

DINOSAURS AND BIRDS

From the dinosaurs came another group of flying creatures: birds. The group of dinosaurs known as theropods (three-toed dinosaurs, which included Tyrannosaurus rex) evolved into birds. The oldest-known bird, *Archaeopteryx lithographica*, is the link between birds and dinosaurs. Archaeopteryx was a feathered bird, but it also had lizard-like features such as a bony tail and teeth.

HELP FROM THE AIR

Looking at pterosaur fossils, some scientists found it difficult to understand how these huge reptiles got off the ground. Although they had thin, hollow bones, they were still heavy and may have had help from the air! During the time of the dinosaurs the air was heavier, or more dense – between 3.5 and 8 times heavier than today. This may have helped the pterosaurs to fly. Turn to page 86 to learn how air helps flight.

PTEROSAUR WINGS

Pterosaur literally means winged lizard. Pterosaurs were not feathered, like birds, but had wings made of muscle and tissue covered by a thin layer of skin, a bit like bats. The enormous wings were supported by little hands. A very long finger stretched out from the hands towards the tips of the wings for support and control.

BIRDS AND BATS

Birds are the most varied group of all flying animals. Their ancestors began flying over 140 million years ago! Their success comes from having hollow bones with air sacs, and a nifty breathing system which allows them to maximise the amount of air inside their bodies at all times. This helps hugely with flight. Bats are the only mammals to have evolved true flight. Some mammals, such as the sugar glider possum, may appear to fly, but really they are gliders.

AIR INSIDE

Birds are so successful at flying because they make use of air both inside and outside their bodies. As well as hollow, lightweight bones, they have a very efficient breathing system. On average, about one-fifth of a bird's body is taken up by its breathing system. In an average mammal, it's only about one-twentieth. Because flight demands more air than walking or running, a bird's super-breathing system is crucial.

THE FRIGATE BIRD HAS A WINGSPAN OF 2.1 M (7 FT), BUT ITS SKELETON WEIGHS EVEN LESS THAN ITS FEATHERS!

BIRD BREATH!

A bird's breathing system is linked to its bones, which are hollow. A bird's lungs are small, but they're connected to a system of air sacs in its body, which are linked to the air spaces in the bones. Air is stored in a bird's body for two breathing cycles. When a bird breathes in, the air doesn't come straight back out when the bird breathes out. Instead, the air travels around the complex breathing system and leaves the body the second time the bird breathes out.

1. First breath in. Air (blue) moves into the air sac.

2. First breath out. Air moves into the lungs.

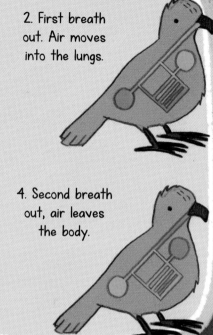

3. Second breath in, air moves into the front air sac.

4. Second breath out, air leaves the body.

BIRD RADAR

When you're flying at top speed, it's very important not to crash! Birds are able to pass messages from eye-to-brain-to-wing at top speed, which helps them fly through the trees with ease. Birds have an excellent nervous system too. They have evolved quick brains and sharp eyes for processing all the information they have to take in. So, as a bird soars through the air at speed, it can swiftly send signals from the brain to the muscles working the wings. All this allows a bird like the peregrine falcon – the fastest animal on Earth – to travel at speeds well over 320 km/h (200 mph)!

BAT WINGS

Scientists think that the bat evolved from a leaping or gliding mammal ancestor, such as the colugo, or flying lemur. Bats have wings made of a fine webbing membrane that stretches between the forelimbs. There is very little fossil evidence of bats, which means the origins of early bats is lost in the mists of time.

UPLIFT!

LIFT IS MOSTLY ASSOCIATED WITH FLIGHT. BUT LIFT IS ALSO MADE BY RUDDERS ON BOATS, SAILS ON SAILBOATS AND 'SPOILERS' ON THE BACK OF RACING CARS!

We've looked at the ways in which pterosaurs, birds and bats were specially adapted to fly. But how did they rise into the air in the first place? The answer is uplift. If you've ever held your hand out ot the window of a moving car you'll have felt the force of air flowing over and above your hand. The moving car makes your hand travel through the air at speed and the air bumps it around! When animals take flight, this movement of air around them is all-important.

CANADA GEESE

These birds fly long distances in winter, spending weeks in the air. They can fly as far as 2,414 km (1,500 mi) in 24 hours. How do they do it?

1. When air hits the front of a wing, it splits to flow both above and below it.

2. The top side of a wing is longer than the bottom side.

3. The air passing above the wing has further to travel than the air passing below, so it needs to move faster to reach the back of the wing at the same time as the air below.

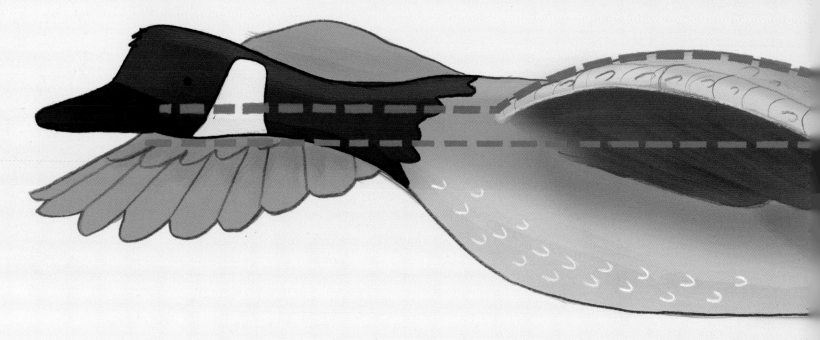

FORCES

When a bird starts flying, air flows past its body and all sorts of natural forces start acting on it. The important force needed for flight is known as 'uplift'. But there is also 'thrust', which is the force with which the bird moves forward, 'weight' which is the force that the bird feels due to gravity and finally 'drag', which is the force the bird feels is holding it back as it flies through the air.

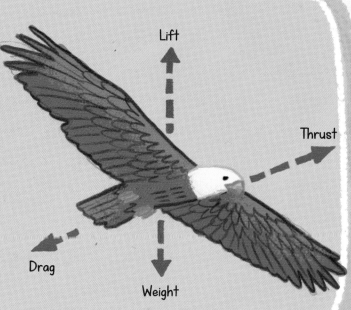

Lift

Thrust

Drag

Weight

4. Because the air moves faster above the wing, the air pressure on top of the wing is less than the pressure on the underside.

5. This causes the wing to be forced upwards, along with the bird.

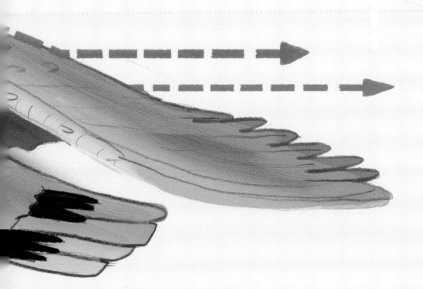

UPLIFT EXPERIMENT

Hold a piece of paper between your thumbs and fingers, as shown below. Take in a big gulp of air and blow over the top of the paper. Do you notice how the paper rises? That's uplift! When you blow over the top, the air moves off the top of the paper and pressure is lost. This means the air pressure underneath the paper is greater than the pressure above, so it pushes the paper up!

THE HISTORY OF FLIGHT

For well over 110 years, humankind has been able to take to the sky. For centuries before that, people tried to understand flight and to fly themselves. In their early attempts, people made wings of feathers or wood and strapped them to their arms. The results were often disastrous! Human muscles simply aren't as strong as birds', and we don't have hollow bones filled with air sacs to help us! Let's take a look at how we finally took to the skies.

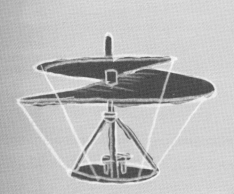

1505

Italian genius Leonardo da Vinci wrote one of the first books about bird flight. Da Vinci also drew detailed inventions for flying machines, including the helicopter and parachute!

1783

Jean-François Pilâtre de Rozier and François Laurent d'Arlandes of France made the first voyage through the air in a hot-air balloon. Unfortunately, de Rozier died in a flight two years later, making him one of the first-known victims of an air crash.

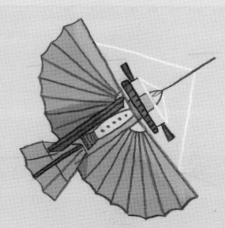

1901

The first powered and manned aircraft may have taken off and landed in America. Gustav Whitehead's 'Number 21' aircraft flew a distance of 800 m (2,620 ft), 15 m (50 ft) above the ground, before landing softly on its wheels again.

1939

German aircraft, the Heinkel 178, became the first fully jet-propelled aircraft to take to the air.

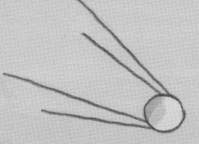

1957

The Soviet Union launched Sputnik 1, the first man-made satellite to orbit Earth.

1961

The Soviet cosmonaut, Yuri Gagarin, became the first human in space.

5TH CENTURY BC

Chinese philosophers Mozi and Lu Ban flew the first kites. They used silk for the sail and the flying line, and **bamboo** for the kite's frame.

400 BC

Archytas, an ancient Greek philosopher, supposedly built a mechanical bird powered by steam, which flew for over 200 m (650 ft).

AD 19

The first record of a person flying is from China. An unnamed person took to the air in a contraption described as being lightly built, with two big wings like those of a bird, and feathers over the head and body. Apparently the flight lasted for a few hundred paces before falling.

1903

The American Wright brothers are often thought to have invented the world's first successful powered, controlled aeroplane. Many people succeeded in taking to the air before the Wright brothers, but they were the first to clearly record and photograph their flights.

1906

1906 saw the first proper flight without the help of external take-off aids (such as rails or catapults). Romanian Trajan Vuia carried out the first flight by a heavier-than-air, self-propelled aircraft.

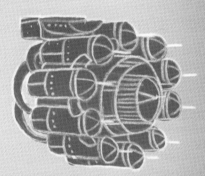

1930

Frank Whittle, a British inventor, invented the jet engine.

TODAY

One of the world's biggest aeroplanes is the Airbus A380. It often carries over 500 passengers and is so big that only 20 runways in the world are long enough to allow it to land.

HOT–AIR BALLOONS

The first flying machines were balloons. This invention made clever use of air rather than trying to mimic bird flight. The air inside a balloon is heated and, as the temperature rises, the molecules within it move away from each other. This causes the volume of air to expand and it becomes less dense than the air around it. The less dense hot air then floats in the more dense cold air, just as wood floats on water (because wood is less dense than water). Bingo, the balloon then takes to the air!

MODERN AEROPLANES

We know that birds have light bones and air sacs in their bodies to enable them to fly with ease. It also makes sense that a kite would fly because the bamboo for the frame weighs next to nothing, and silk or paper is easily lifted by the wind. But how do huge, heavy planes carrying hundreds of people climb into the sky and actually stay up there? Here's the science behind these amazing metal birds!

ANYONE FOR A LIFT?

Turn back to pages 86-87 to remind yourself about uplift and remember the experiment with a piece of paper. When air is blown over the top, pressure is lost, and the greater air pressure underneath pushes the paper up. The same science applies to aeroplanes. But the weight of an aeroplane is much greater than a piece of paper! So a plane has to charge down the runway, gathering enough speed to move the air above its wings. Once the force of uplift is greater than the weight of the aeroplane, the plane lifts into the air.

ANGLE OF ATTACK

To help it achieve uplift, an aeroplane's wings are shaped and tilted. The wing shape is known as its 'angle of attack'. That's the angle that the front of the wing has as it faces the oncoming air. People have learnt that the greater the angle of attack, the greater the lift. And the smaller the angle, the less the lift. It seems obvious but it's actually easier for an aeroplane to climb into the air than it is to keep it cruising at a steady speed.

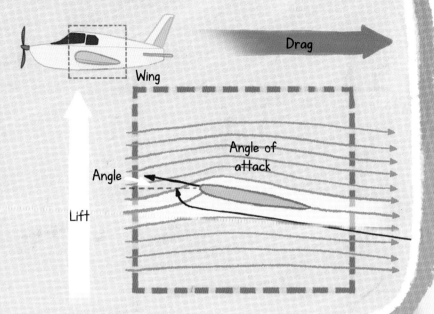

JET ENGINES

To stay in the air, a plane needs to balance the forces of weight and drag, otherwise it won't move forward and will fall to the ground. We know how uplift works, but a plane also needs thrust to start moving. Large passenger planes have jet engines that make use of the air to help them speed along. These engines use a 'jet' of air to help with thrust. Air is swallowed up at the front of the engine. Then the air is squeezed through the engine, fuel is added, and the mixture is burnt (called combustion). See page 154 for more information about this. A jet engine thrusts the hot exhaust gases out of the back of the engine. In reaction, an equal thrusting force is produced in the opposite direction which moves the plane forwards.

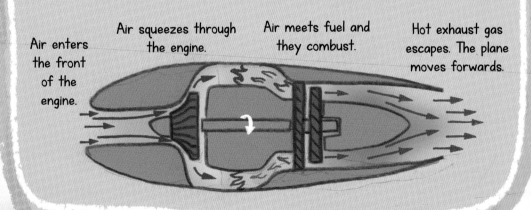

Air enters the front of the engine.

Air squeezes through the engine.

Air meets fuel and they combust.

Hot exhaust gas escapes. The plane moves forwards.

SIGNPOSTS IN THE SKY

Have you ever wondered how many people are flying at any one given time? Data tells us that over 3 billion passengers take around 25 million flights each year. Analysts looking at the data know that the average flight duration is two hours, and so they've worked out that there are up to 700,000 people in the sky at any one time. It's getting crowded up there!

AIR TRAFFIC CONTROL

The air has become heavy with traffic. But without roads to stick to, the job of keeping everyone safe lies with air traffic control. A group of people on the ground, called air traffic control, direct the movements of thousands of aircraft in the sky. At peak air travel times in the USA, there are more than 50,000 aircraft flying across the country each day. Air traffic control keeps planes at safe distances from each other, assists during take-off and landing and advises when bad weather is on its way. Air traffic control have had a good day at work when everything flies smoothly and there are no delays or crashes!

PATHWAYS TO FLY

In an ideal world, aeroplanes would always fly the most direct route between two points, to get passengers there quickly and use the minimum amount of fossil fuel. The direct route from A to B on a sphere (like our planet) is known as the great circle distance. But flights sometimes have to stray away from this route. Take the flight from New York to Singapore for example: the great circle route goes over the North Pole. But instead planes fly longer routes north or south of the great circle to pick up stronger winds, and to be near airports in case of an emergency. Planes may also divert from the great circle route because of traffic in the sky, bad weather or sometimes there are war zones or no-fly zones along a route.

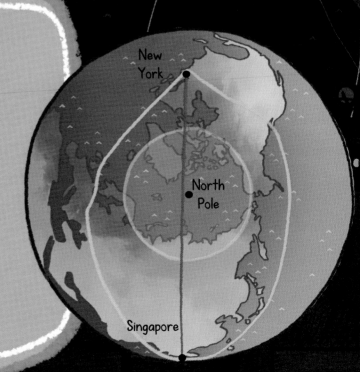

New York

North Pole

Singapore

—— Most direct route   —— Actual routes flown by planes

WEATHER DELAYS

Let's look at the North Pacific great circle air route from the west coast of America to China. From the USA, the aeroplane would head northwest to Alaska, then south to China. But if the winds are blowing strongly against the plane, it's faster to fly a more southerly route, even though it is a longer distance. Sometimes storms like typhoons (see page 125) in the Pacific Ocean mean planes must change course to avoid them.

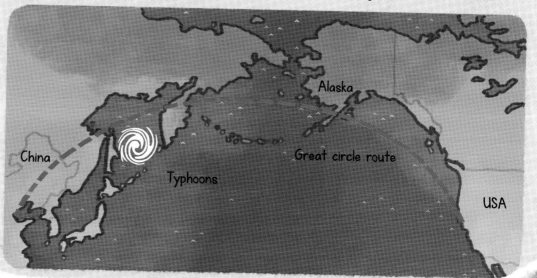

China

Alaska

Typhoons

Great circle route

USA

AIRSPACE ZONES

There are thousands of air traffic control groups, but they can't all watch the entire globe at once, so the air above our planet is divided into zones. Each zone has its own square area to watch over and ensure safety. Each group works within a zone and has different categories of controllers.

INTO SPACE

The story of human flight doesn't end on Earth. Our mastery of flight has taken us from the air in our atmosphere out into the black of outer space. We've gone one step further than nature's flying creatures! Scientists worked out what was needed to break through the layers of air and out into space: rockets! Space travel involves rocket science, but your rocket doesn't have to be the most complex thing in the world. You could reach space with a rocket the size of a telegraph pole just by going really, really fast!

ESCAPE!

All you need to leave Earth behind you is the right escape speed. That means the speed you need to travel to escape the pull of Earth's gravity. Like most engines, rockets work by burning fuel and converting it into gas. A rocket's engine pushes the gas out of its back end, and this is what creates the thrust that moves the rocket in a certain direction.

JET ENGINE VS ROCKET ENGINE

A jet engine's fuel can only burn by using oxygen from the air it flies through. But a rocket engine must work in space, where there is no oxygen. So, a rocket must carry its own oxygen. Rockets that use liquid fuel have tanks of liquid oxygen, while solid-fuelled rockets carry fuel that contains a chemical with oxygen mixed in.

4. The main fuel tank burns up, detaches, then burns out on re-entry into the atmosphere.

2. The initial fuel tank rockets burn out and detach.

3. The tanks deploy parachutes so they will slowly drift back down to Earth.

1. Rockets launch the spacecraft into the air.

SITTING PRETTY

Travelling from Earth into space is a piece of cake. But to stay up there and not fall back to Earth, or to continue on to another planet, you have to travel at a speed of about 8 km (5 mi) per SECOND! So your spacecraft has to move at 28,000 km/h (17,500 mph) just to stay in orbit around the Earth or continue its journey.

5. The spacecraft enters orbit above Earth.

6. The crew carry out their mission.

7. The spacecraft breaks out of the orbit cycle.

8. The spacecraft re-enters the Earth's atmosphere.

IT'S A DRAG

When a spacecraft returns to Earth, the atmosphere makes its presence felt. As gravity pulls the spacecraft down, the vehicle falls through the layers of atmosphere and creates friction. This friction, or 'drag' as it's called when in the air, is made by the spacecraft rubbing up against all those particles of air. This causes so much heat that spacecraft have to be designed to withstand temperatures as great as 1,650°C (3,000°F)!

9. The spacecraft lands back on Earth.

HUMANS AND AIR

All human beings need to breathe air to stay alive. But how does air find its way into our bodies and how do we extract the oxygen from it so it can be of use? An average person breathes in and out more than 20,000 times in a day, so let's follow the journey of a single breath of air.

NOSE, SINUSES AND WINDPIPE

Air enters your body through your nose and mouth, then travels down your windpipe, known as the trachea, and into your lungs. Your nose, containing tiny bristly hairs and mucus, helps filter out dust and other particles in the air as it enters your body. Your nose and sinuses also keep the incoming air warm and moist, so it doesn't dry out your sensitive lungs.

ENTER THE LUNGS

Your lungs are the centre of the breathing process and act like pumps, or bellows. You have two lungs, but the left one is slightly smaller to make room for your heart. Underneath your lungs is a big muscle called the diaphragm. Your diaphragm moves up and down to control breathing in and out. When this muscle tightens you take in a breath and air rushes into your lungs. A big breath of air brings about a hundred quintillion (100,000,000,000,000,000,000) molecules of oxygen into your body.

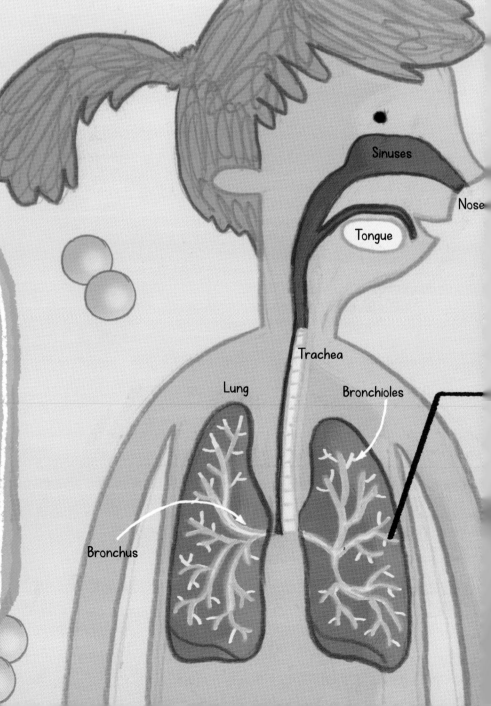

Sinuses

Nose

Tongue

Trachea

Lung

Bronchioles

Bronchus

AIR INTO THE BLOOD

Your lungs are like an upside-down tree. The trunk is the trachea and the two main branches of the tree are called bronchi. They branch off into smaller, narrower tubes called bronchioles, which end in tiny ducts and sacs called alveoli. At these sacs oxygen molecules dissolve and enter the blood stream. Alveoli are also where carbon dioxide leaves the blood and follows the same journey in reverse to get out of your body, via the mouth and nose.

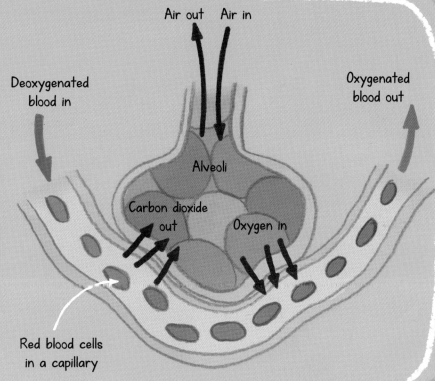

Air out Air in

Deoxygenated blood in

Oxygenated blood out

Alveoli

Carbon dioxide out

Oxygen in

Red blood cells in a capillary

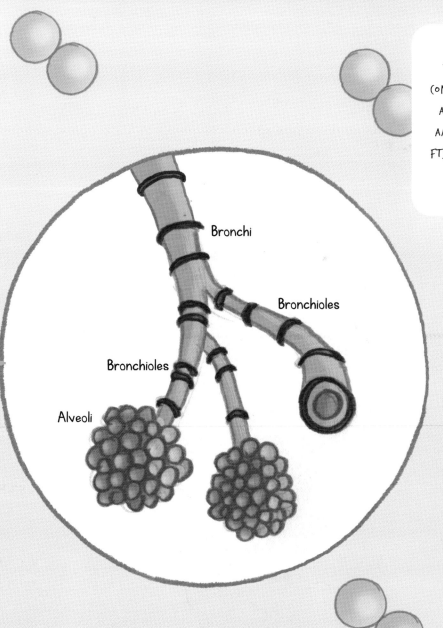

Bronchi

Bronchioles

Bronchioles

Alveoli

TOGETHER YOUR LUNGS CONTAIN ABOUT 300 MILLION ALVEOLI. THEY MAKE AN AMAZING 75 SQ M (800 SQ FT) OF MOIST SURFACE AREA FOR BREATHING!

AROUND THE BODY

Once your blood cells have picked up oxygen from the lungs, they travel to the heart, which then pumps them around the body. Red blood cells pass oxygen and other essential chemicals to your organs and muscles so that they can function and operate your body!

SOUND

Imagine what it would be like living without sound. You wouldn't hear the thousands of noises going on around you every day. You wouldn't hear people talking, or music, or birds singing. Most people never really experience complete silence, even for a minute. Sound is always all around us in the air, but how does it work? To help you picture it, imagine sound is like a wave rippling through water.

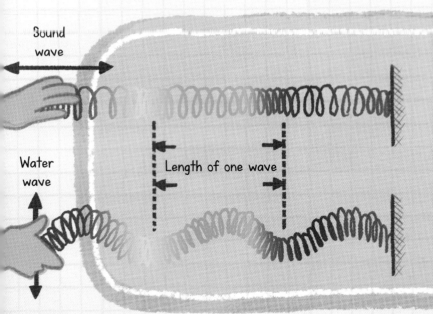

Sound wave

Water wave

Length of one wave

SOUND WAVES

Sound travels in waves, but sound waves are different to water waves. Water waves travel along the surface, moving up and down as the water flows forwards. Sound waves travel lengthwise, shaking the molecules around them. Sounds can travel through solids (such as metal), liquids (water) and gases (air), vibrating molecules as they pass through. When the object vibrates, the vibrations enter your ear and you hear sound!

HOW SOUND WORKS

Imagine a mobile phone receiving a message. The TING noise is made by the phone's mini loudspeaker, which is a tiny disc-shaped device, called a diaphragm. When the phone makes the diaphragm move back and forth, it vibrates the air around your phone. That makes the particles of air move back and forth and this creates the 'ting' noise you hear.

Ting!

PUSHED AND PULLED

When sound travels through air, sound waves make air molecules come together (compress) and then spread apart (expand). Sound pushes and pulls the air back and forth, making a wave-like pattern. The waves can be big or small. Big sound waves make a loud noise because they have a high **amplitude**. Wavelength measures the distance between each sound wave.

Air molecules

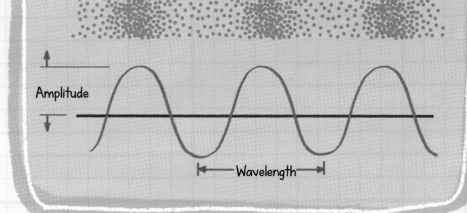

Amplitude

Wavelength

PITCH

For many centuries, people described different types of sound in terms of pitch. A high sound, such as a squeaking mouse, has a high pitch. A low sound, such as a roaring tiger, has a low pitch. That's because the mouse makes many more sound waves per second, than the tiger.

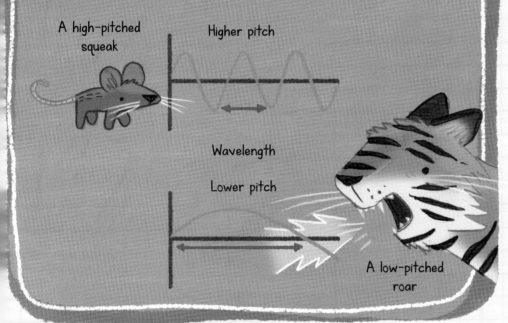

A high-pitched squeak

Higher pitch

Wavelength

Lower pitch

A low-pitched roar

LOUDNESS

The other important quality of sound is loudness. Loudness is how loud or soft a sound is. A loud sound has a high amplitude whereas a quiet sound has a low amplitude. Sound waves die out when they travel over distance So the further you are from the source of a wave, the quieter it sounds. There's a range of sound wave intensities that people can comfortably hear. Among the loudest are sound waves close to a large loudspeaker.

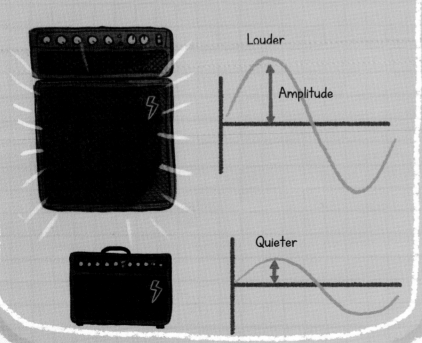

Louder

Amplitude

Quieter

LOUDNESS SCALE

Sound is measured in **decibels**, or dB. The higher the number in decibels, the louder the noise.

140 dB: jet plane taking off
(Anything above this level of loudness will damage your hearing permanently.)

120 dB: rock concert

105 dB: MP3 player turned up to maximum level

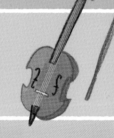

95 dB: large orchestra playing

85 dB: street traffic

75 dB: vacuum cleaner

65 dB: normal conversation

20 dB: whisper

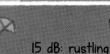

15 dB: rustling leaves

SPEECH

To understand how speech evolved, let's try to imagine what it was like for the first human beings on our planet. We know they were hunter-gatherers who tracked and hunted animals for food. It must have been very tough - things like sudden noises and stormy weather would have startled **grazing** animals and made them even more difficult to catch. It may be that our ancestors learnt to recognise the signs of a storm brewing (dark skies and a rising wind) and knew that this would scare away animals. Perhaps they created a set of grunts and gestures to warn others a storm was on the way and to speed up the hunt. It could be that these grunts were the start of speech!

SPEAKING AND LISTENING

Our bodies have developed the ability to make speech sounds, and also to be able to hear and understand them. Noise is made by letting air out through the larynx (see the next panel) and mouth. We create different sounds by using parts of our mouth and throat to change the shape of sound waves: our vocal cords, tongue, teeth, upper mouth and lips all play a part in this. Try moving your lips as you hum to see how this affects the sound! Our ears pick up sound waves created by other people and send signals to the brain to interpret them.

HOW SPEECH WORKS

Your windpipe (or trachea) is a tube that leads from your throat down to your lungs. At the top of the windpipe is your voice box (or larynx). The larynx contains two bands of tissue called your vocal cords. When you breathe, your vocal cords move apart and are fully open. But when you speak or sing, these cords come together and close up. This causes the vocal cords to become stretched and tight. So now, when air is let out from the lungs, it passes over the tight cords and they vibrate, creating sound.

Vocal cords close when speaking

Vocal cords

Vocal cords open when breathing

Vocal cords

Larynx

HIGH AND LOW

The shorter your vocal cords are, and the faster they vibrate, the higher pitched your speech will be.

VOICE BOX CHANGES

During puberty, the human voice box and vocal cords grow. This means they get longer so the sounds coming out of them get deeper. In boys, this growth can be quite considerable, meaning their voices deepen dramatically and their larynx may start to be a visible bump in their neck – this is called an 'Adam's Apple'.

LANGUAGE

Way back in early human history, our ancestors began to create a system of speech sounds that helped them survive. Some scientists think that every language on the planet today - from Mandarin to English - evolved from one single, ancient language first spoken in Africa at least 100,000 years ago. Language spread around the globe when early humans began to migrate out of Africa roughly 70,000 years ago.

Inuit: 22
(Greenland)

COUNTING SOUNDS

One theory is that we can follow the journey of language out of Africa by counting the number of phonemes (units of sound) each language uses. Scientists have done this for over 500 languages from different parts of the globe, and noted them on a map. The number of phonemes varies greatly from language to language. For example, English has around 46 phonemes, but some South American languages have fewer than 15. The San Bushmen of southern Africa use an astounding 200 phonemes.

Hawaiian: 13

Warao: 21
(Venezuela)

Piraha: 11
(Brazil)

UNITS OF SOUND

A phoneme is the smallest unit of sound. In English this can be an individual letter (e.g. 'b' or 'c'), a pair of letters (e.g. 'sh' or 'oo') or even three letters (e.g. 'igh' or 'ure'). So, the sounds made by saying the letters 'b' and 'c' represent different phonemes. This is what makes the words 'bat' and 'cat' sound different even though two of their three letters are the same.

OUT OF AFRICA

You can see from the map that the number of different sounds (or phonemes) in a native language increases the closer it is to Africa. These differences in numbers may echo the migration paths of our ancestors (see pages 56-65). This is because language changes as it is handed down through the generations – you probably don't use certain words your grandparents did. When our ancestors first started migrating around the world, a large group, such as the early people who remained in southern Africa, probably had quite a constant language. That's because there were a lot of people who could remember all the words and sounds. The people who journeyed out of Africa split into smaller groups, and each group had different experiences. Each group probably dropped words they didn't use and created new ones to reflect their day-to-day lives.

Russian: 38

English: 46

German: 41

French: 37

Archi: 91
(Dagestan, Russia)

Kurdish: 47 (Iraq)

Farsi: 30 (Iran)

Mandarin: 32 (China)

Korean: 32

Japanese: 20

Bodo: 21
(Northeast India)

Bengali: 43

Tagalog: 23
(Philippines)

Dahalo: 59
(Kenya)

Roro: 14
(Papua New Guinea)

San: 200
(Southern Africa)

Xu: 141
(South Africa)

Bandjalang: 16
(Australia)

SOUNDS ARE LIKE GENES

Sounds in languages are like the genes we talked about on pages 52-55 of this book (though of course languages evolve much faster than genes). Native Africans today have a much greater diversity of genes than native white Europeans for example.

CREATURE SOUNDS

Have you ever wished you could talk to a tiger? Or wondered what it might be like to chat with a chimpanzee or rant at a rhinoceros? Though we cannot understand much of what an animal says or does, we know communication plays a vital role in the lives of all animals. One of the main ways animals communicate is using sound. The sounds animals make are much more varied than humans, as they cover a wider range of loudness, length and pitch.

The 'eagle' alarm call makes the monkeys dive into bushes or the middle of trees where an aerial predator can't reach them.

MONKEY BUSINESS

Monkeys are clever communicators. Vervet monkeys, who originate from southeast Africa, use alarm sounds to warn other group members about looming predators. The sounds even suggest what actions fellow monkeys should take. For example, a 'cough' call means there is a predator in the air above. All monkeys hearing this know to dive for cover in the thick vegetation on the ground. A different noise is used if a ground predator, such as a leopard, is stalking the colony.

The 'snake' alarm call causes the group to stand up and study the ground.

NOT SO BATTY

Bats have poor eyesight but they have developed a very clever way of using sound to hunt. They emit very high-pitched sounds, which travel outwards and bounce back when they hit an object. This is called echolocation, because the sound waves bounce back, just like an echo. The bat listens for the sound wave to bounce back and by calculating how long it takes, the bat can work out exactly where it is, what is around it, and most importantly, where its prey is!

ANIMAL TRICKS

Animal 'speech' happens when one member of a species makes a noise that is understood by another. But this may not always go according to plan. For example, male túngara frogs make mating calls to attract females. But eavesdropping fringe-lipped bats can also pick up the frog's calls and use the sounds to locate the frogs and gobble them up!

The 'leopard' alarm call sends individuals scuttling up to the tops of the trees.

SOUND IN WATER

Sound waves travel through solids and liquids as well as air, so creatures under water can communicate too. Male humpback whales make incredibly varied sounds, ranging from high-pitched squeaks to low, burbling grumbles. The whales are also well known for their magical songs, which travel over great distances through the sea. The symphony of sounds they make are complex, and last for hours at a time. It is believed that the humpbacks sing to 'talk' to each other, and for males to attract females.

MUSIC

Music is what happens when the air vibrates in a regular way - it's a pattern of sounds. These patterns of air vibrations can be made by the human voice, by musical instruments, computers, or even a combination of all three. We believe that between 40,000 and 100,000 years ago, humans took a creative leap when they began to create art such as cave paintings and jewellery. It's possible they also began to make music around the same time.

CALL OF THE WILD

Scientists have different theories about why our ancestors first started making music. Some believe music began when early people copied the cries of animals, and then used these calls as a kind of mating call between men and women. The regular sound patterns they made would have been enjoyable to listen to. By copying the calls of nature, early humans introduced tone, clicks, whistles and humming into their musical habits. Why don't you try humming or whistling a tune!

MUSIC AND SPEECH

Music is similar to speech, especially in languages used in some parts of Africa, and Asia, such as Zulu, Chinese and Vietnamese. These 'tonal' languages use tone and pitch to portray the meaning of words, as much as the words themselves. In fact, the same word can be said in different tonal ways to make different meanings. So we can begin to imagine that speech and music may have developed together.

EARLY INSTRUMENTS

The first instruments created by our ancestors were made of stone, wood, horn and bone. Stone Age cave art, dating back 35,000 years ago, shows people playing primitive flutes. There is cave art from 10,000 years ago showing a man playing a musical bow. He holds one end of the string in his mouth, and he plucks the other end. These musical bows are still played by people in several African cultures today.

THE DRUM

One of the earliest instruments was the drum. A slit drum was carved out of wood to create a box with one or more slits in the top. Other types of drum were made by simply stretching animal skins over wooden bowls, or frames. These drums make sounds when a stick, or hand, is struck down hard on the skin or hole. It vibrates the material, and then the air, to make sound waves which are echoed in the hollow space within.

INSTRUMENTS

When people play music, aside from using our voices, we blow, bang or strum! A modern orchestra is a group of instruments played together, and is usually made of four sections: the woodwind, brass, string and percussion. The woodwind and brass sections include instruments that you blow into, such as the clarinet, trumpet and flute. Stringed instruments, such as the violin, produce sound when their strings are plucked or strummed, or have a bow drawn across them. The huge range of percussion instruments all need to be hit or shaken in some way to make a noise.

THE FIRST INSTRUMENTS

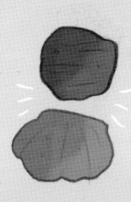

c.60,000 BC

Stone Age people were the first to make music. They created the first cave art and made the first music. Their early instruments would have been percussion instruments made from bone, sticks, rocks and shells hit together.

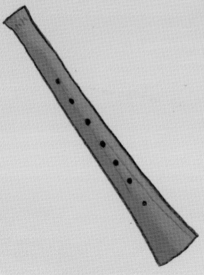

35,000 BC

People living in Hohel Fels caves in what is modern-day Germany made flutes from the wing-bones of vultures and mammoth ivory.

2500 BC

In the city-state of Ur, in ancient Mesopotamia (present-day Iraq, parts of Turkey and Syria), musicians played stringed instruments such as the harp and lute.

1000 BC

Chinese instruments such as bells, chimes and a mouth organ known as the sheng appeared around 3,000 years ago.

THE FIRST FLUTE

Many wind instruments developed from the first flute. The flute's sound is made by vibrating a column of air inside the tube. A melody is created when the player changes the pitch, which depends on the volume of air vibrating inside. From ancient times, musicians altered the pitch by opening and closing holes along the length of the instrument. Closing holes means the air has fewer places to exit the instrument, so the column of air is bigger. More vibrating air creates lower notes.

THE FIRST STRINGS

The harp was one of the first stringed instruments. It makes a sound when plucked strings vibrate and move the air around them. The lute makes sounds in a similar way, but it has a body with a long neck, and a soundboard, which helps make the sound from the vibrating strings louder.

SHENG

The sheng is a mouth-blown instrument made of vertical wooden pipes. Reeds inside the pipes vibrate when air is blown over them. The player of the sheng both blows and inhales air, making a continuous sound without gaps.

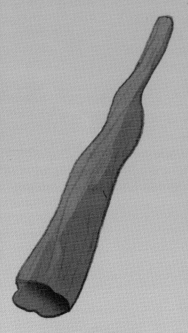

AD 500

Aboriginal people in Australia developed the didgeridoo, a long wooden instrument that looks like a hollow pole.

1200

Early guitars appeared in Spain. These instruments had strings stretched over a hollow box. When strummed, the vibrations caused by the strings were made louder by the guitar's hollow body

1530

The violin was developed in northern Italy. The violin is 'strummed' by drawing a bow across the strings rather than plucking. The sound of a violin depends on its shape, the wood it's made from and its thickness.

1700

The piano is a stringed instrument whose strings are struck, rather than strummed. Hammers strike the piano strings, activated by black and white keys on the keyboard. The large wooden body of the piano acts as a speaker by passing the noise made by the string vibrations into the air.

DIDGERIDOO

The didgeridoo is an interesting instrument to play. To make a continuous noise from it, the player must constantly vibrate their lips whilst breathing in through the nose, and out through the mouth. The player's lips and breath cause the column of air inside the instrument to vibrate at various frequencies. But the sound waves also travel up into the player's vocal tract. So, by changing things like the shape and position of the tongue, different notes and pitches can be made. In some ways, the didgeridoo plays the person!

WEATHER AND CLIMATE

Take a look at the weather outside your window. Is it the same as yesterday, or different? Weather is local and short-term: maybe it will snow heavily in your part of the world tomorrow but melt and disappear a couple of days later. Climate, however, is long-term and global. Climate isn't about the weather in one place, but about typical weather conditions in a large region over a long period of time. In fact, changes in climate can take tens of thousands of years, or longer.

WHAT AFFECTS CLIMATE?

Climate change is a complicated business. It can take our planet thousands of years to warm up by just one degree. As well as the cycles of the ice ages (see pages 200-201), Earth's climate can be influenced by volcanoes, plant life, the amount of sunlight and changes in the amounts of different gases in the atmosphere.

CLIMATE SWINGS

For the past million years, Earth's climate has been swinging back and forth between long periods of cold climate (ice ages), and much shorter periods of warm climate. The changes have happened because of small variations in the Earth's orbit around the Sun. These variations influence the amount of heat falling on different parts of the Earth's atmosphere and surface.

During an ice age, much of the Earth is covered in ice.

HUMAN FACTOR

If the swinging pattern of warm and cold climate change had continued as expected, we would now be heading into a new ice age. The ice would have crept down from the poles and smothered much of the land once again. Temperatures would have started falling about 7,000 years ago. But we are not in an ice age today... there is only ice at the poles of our planet. This is because of the human impact on Earth.

FARMING AFFECTS THE AIR

One theory is that just when the climate should have been cooling, farming really took off. Farming began around 11,000 years ago (see page 42) and by 7,000 years ago, it had a huge impact on the planet. More methane gases entered the atmosphere because of greater numbers of domesticated animals (which burp and fart methane!), and more carbon dioxide was released as more trees were cut down. These two factors changed the natural balance of the air and may have contributed towards temperatures remaining steady, instead of falling. Human beings may have stalled the next ice age.

CLIMATE CHANGE

Human influence on the atmosphere and our planet has increased over recent years. Thousands of scientists from countries across the world agree that between 1906 and 2006, our planet's average temperature increase was 0.74°C (1.4°F).

Since the year 2000, we've had 15 out of 17 of the hottest years on record.

The rate at which the climate is warming up has doubled in the past 50 years.

There have been big changes in temperature patterns around the globe – hot days and heat waves have become more common. Cold days have become less common.

WIND AND AIR

The air above our heads is rarely still. We feel changes in the air as wind. Wind is created by currents of air that ebb and flow a bit like oceans. Winds can be both local and global. The main flow of global wind happens because the regions at the Earth's equator get more heat from the Sun than those at the poles. The warmed air rises, then it cools and sinks, forming a flow of air around the globe. This is how a circulation cycle is formed around our planet.

The global circulation of surface air sits in three main belts both above and below the equator. They are...

The polar easterlies

SWIRLING WINDS

The Earth is constantly spinning in an anti-clockwise direction. We don't feel the movement but we see it in the form of day and night! The Earth spins on an axis that runs from the North Pole, through the centre, down to the South Pole, like a spinning top. And it is partly this spinning that makes the winds swirl.

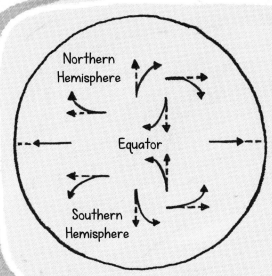

THE CORIOLIS EFFECT

Because the Earth is spinning, the flow of air around it is deflected to the right in a clockwise cycle in the Northern Hemisphere and to the left in an anti-clockwise cycle in the Southern Hemisphere. This makes the wind flow on curved paths and scientists call this flow the Coriolis effect. The Coriolis effect means that the flow in the three main cycles of air is turned into winds called 'easterlies' and 'westerlies'.

IF THE EARTH DIDN'T SPIN, THE AIR WOULD ONLY CIRCULATE BETWEEN THE POLES AND THE EQUATOR IN A CIRCLE.

AIR MASSES

Air masses are huge volumes of air that sit over certain areas on the Earth's surface. As they move around the globe, they tend to take their particular characteristics with them too. This means these volumes of air keep the same temperature and humidity that they had when they were created. The four main classes of air mass are:

Equatorial (E), Tropical (T), Polar (P) and Arctic (A). The classes can also be written with another lowercase letter, which shows whether the air began over a continental (over land) or maritime (over water) area on Earth's surface.

The mid-latitude westerlies

The tropical easterlies

continental Polar (cP)
Formed in polar regions, it blows over the land so it is dry and cool

continental Arctic (cA)
Formed in the Arctic circle, it is very dry and very cold

maritime Polar (mP)
Formed in polar regions, it blows over the sea so it is moist and cool

maritime Tropical (mT)
Formed in subtropical ocean regions, it is very moist and warm

continental Tropical (cT)
Formed in subtropical land regions, it is very dry and warm

maritime Equatorial (mE)
Formed over warm seas at the equator, it is very moist and hot

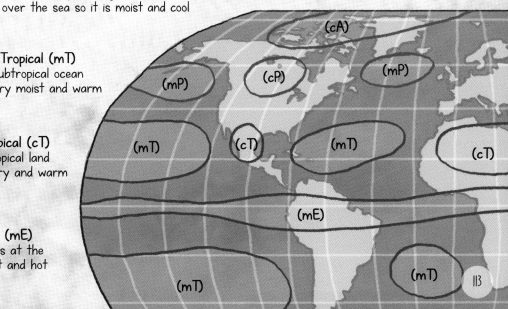

CLOUD SPOTTING

(CLOUDS ARE PART OF THE WATER CYCLE – TURN TO PAGES 194–195 TO READ ABOUT THIS PROCESS.

Look up in the sky and, wherever you are in the world, it's very likely you'll see a cloud! Do you ever wonder how high up you'd have to go to reach it? And if you could touch it, what would it feel like? Those huge, white fluffy clouds, which often look like cotton wool, are actually made up of lots of tiny, floating drops of water. In fact, nearly all weather is made of wind and water. Clouds, wind, fog, rain and snow all contain water.

WATER IN THE AIR

The amount of water in the atmosphere changes. It can be as high as 4%, but at other times the air might be totally dry. As the temperature of the air increases, so too does the amount of water it can hold.

At the highest level, cirrus clouds are entirely made up of ice crystals.

In the middle zone you'll find altostratus and altocumulus clouds.

Cirrus

Cirrocumulus

Cirrostratus

Altocumulus

HIGH CLOUDS

CLOUD SYMBOLS

If you decide to go out cloud spotting, it's also quite handy to learn the shorthand symbols for each cloud type, so you can quickly and easily make a note of them as you watch the sky. The main types of cloud, along with some sub-types, each have their own special symbol.

CLOUD TYPES

Clouds appear in lots of shapes and sizes. With a little practice, a cloud spotter can learn to recognise the main types. We split clouds up into three kinds:

stratus = layered clouds
cumulus = heaped clouds
cirrus = feathery clouds

Knowing the type of cloud also gives you a better idea of how high in the air the cloud is. Clouds occur at three different heights in the troposphere:

low clouds = below 2,000 m (6,500 ft)
medium clouds = 2–6,000 m (6.5–20,000 ft)
high clouds = above 6,000 m (20,000 ft)

CLOUDS IN ALL ZONES

Some cloud types tend to sit in just one of the three zones, while others can be very deep. For instance, cumulonimbus clouds may run from the lowest zone, right up to the highest level of the troposphere.

Stratus clouds are found closer to the ground. They are low-lying clouds and fog.

MEDIUM CLOUDS

Altostratus

Cumulonimbus

Stratocumulus

Cumulus

Nimbostratus

Stratus

LOW CLOUDS

EL NIÑO

In late 1997, the weather was suddenly a bit weird in different places around the world. California in the USA, which is normally a dry place, received record rainfall, causing rivers to burst their banks and flood the land, damaging houses and blocking busy roads. The water running off the mountains there created rivers of mud that flowed through many neighbourhoods. However, across the Pacific Ocean, in Southeast Asia, the exact opposite was taking place - there wasn't enough rain. Dozens of wildfires scorched the dry land and the resulting thick smoke clogged up the air and turned daylight to dusk. The problem in both places was because of a weather-effect taking place in the Pacific Ocean called El Niño.

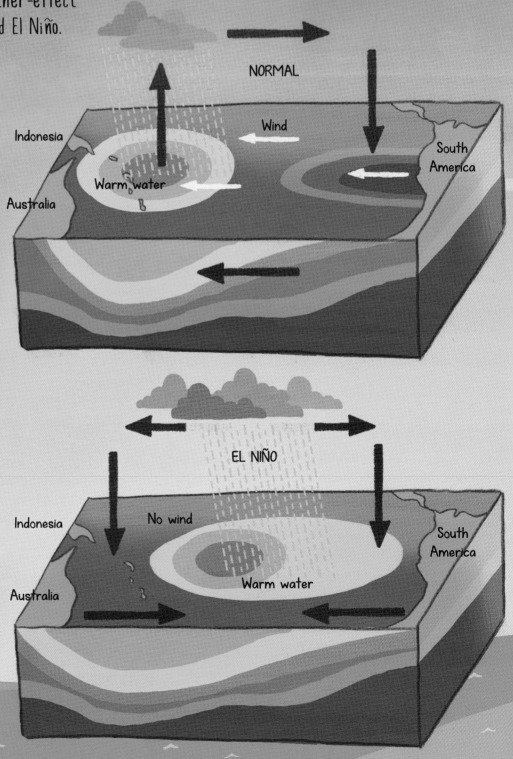

HOW IT HAPPENS

The world's weather depends a lot on the wind and the oceans. Where the water is warm, more clouds form and rain falls. The El Niño effect happens when winds that usually push warm water at the equator towards Indonesia die down or suddenly change direction. Scientists are not exactly sure what triggers this, but it may be to do with the spinning of the Earth and the waves created in the oceans. The wind change allows the warm water to spread out towards South America. The usually cool waters by the coast heat up and create more clouds and more rain.

Warm El Niño waters

FOOD AND HEALTH

El Niño changes the normal wind and weather patterns around the world. A small change in the Pacific Ocean winds can have a knock-on effect to other wind and water cycles nearby, which then affect other cycles near them, and so on, until locations far away from the original event are affected. El Niño also has a major effect on the food and health of people living in these areas.

In an area that usually receives a lot of rainfall, a sudden drought can kill the crops growing there.

El Niño can be bad for human health, too, as unusually wet and warm conditions create a boom in disease-carrying insects and rodents.

WHEN AND FOR HOW LONG?

El Niño happens every two to seven years, and scientists can usually predict its arrival up to six months in advance. The change in wind can last for 9 to 24 months.

THE COST

With all the floods, fires, storms and mudslides that El Niño creates, its effects can be costly. By the time the weather event at the end of 1997 had finished, around $33 billion of damage had been caused.

READING THE AIR

Navigation is the science of planning and directing a journey. On land, it's easy to take a note of your surroundings, but at sea everything looks the same, so it was difficult for early sailors to work out where they were. Today, navigation at sea works by using positions of latitude and longitude (see pages 220-221), but before that sailors had to rely on their observations of the stars and weather. The Vikings, who lived from roughly 700 to 1100, were experts at reading the conditions and using their knowledge of them to sail the seas.

AT ONE WITH NATURE

How did the Vikings navigate their way across the water? They observed the wind, weather and wildlife, and were keen watchers of the sky. The Vikings were fishermen and farmers so they had a deep understanding of nature. They used the Sun, and mapped the position of the stars to track their location. When it was foggy or cloudy, they estimated their location by bird watching. Some birds never fly far from land, and so recognising these birds helped Viking sailors work out if they were close to places they knew.

THE VIKINGS WERE A GROUP OF PEOPLE LIVING IN WHAT IS NOW SCANDINAVIA. THEY WERE SEAFARERS AND SAILED TO NORTHERN AND SOUTHERN EUROPE, AND TO GREENLAND AND NORTH AMERICA.

THE SENSES

Vikings used four of their five senses to help them navigate and pilot their boats. By listening out for screeching birds, and the sound of waves breaking on the shore, Viking sailors could hear how close they were to land. They used their sense of touch to work out the direction and speed of the wind as it blew across their faces. They picked up the scent of trees, plants and even fire from some distance away and so could smell land. Finally, they watched subtle changes in the weather and the clouds above, which helped them identify the wind direction.

FIRST ACROSS THE LINE

The Vikings' navigational know-how in unexplored waters meant they were the first Europeans to visit America. They arrived around the year 1000, beating Christopher Columbus by almost 500 years (see pages 218-219).

THE BAROMETER

Today, a device called a barometer can help us to read the air by measuring air pressure. When air pressure is high it generally means fair weather. When the pressure is low it means stormy weather is coming. The first barometer was created in 1644 by an Italian named Evangelista Torricelli.

CHINA ⟨AND⟩ THE WIND

Sometimes wind can influence the course of human history. The ancient Chinese civilisation owes much of its success to a type of soil called loess. This rich, yellow, dust-like soil is made of many layers of fine sediment, or silt, that is carried on high winds and deposited on Chinese land. Over thousands of years, layers build up to form the soil. In ancient China high winds picked up this rich, silty dust from desert regions and deposited it on a **plateau**, creating rich farmland. This area became the cradle of the ancient Chinese civilisation.

WIND OVER THE HIMALAYAS

The winds that create the loess come from India. Millions of years ago, when the tectonic plate of land that is now India collided with the Asian plate, the Himalayan Mountains were created. They are the highest mountains in the world. Because they are so huge, they affect the air around them and create new wind patterns. When the winds reach the far side of the Himalayas they pick up and move dry loess dust and mineral particles onto the central plateau of China. The Chinese then use this rich loess soil to grow their crops.

Himalayas

Wind

LOESS SOIL

Loess is no ordinary dust, it is rich in minerals. When it combines with plant matter it forms a light, fertile soil perfect for growing crops in – read more about soil on page 20. The Chinese loess originates up high on the central plateau in China. Because the weather is very dry up here, the loess sits in the soil rather than being washed away and piles up to more than 91 m (300 ft) thick in places. When the wind blows, it acts like a huge conveyor belt blowing the loess soil all around China. This is why China was one of the first places in the world to cultivate rice, as they had the perfect soil for it to grow in.

THE TERRACOTTA ARMY

The ancient Chinese civilisation developed on a colossal scale, largely thanks to the extra food they were able to grow to feed the population. Around 770 BC, construction of the Great Wall of China began across the northern border of the Chinese empire. When the First Emperor of China died in 210 BC, he was buried in this area along with a terracotta army to protect him. This army is a huge collection of sculptures, buried within the loess. The terracotta from which they are made is also made from loess!

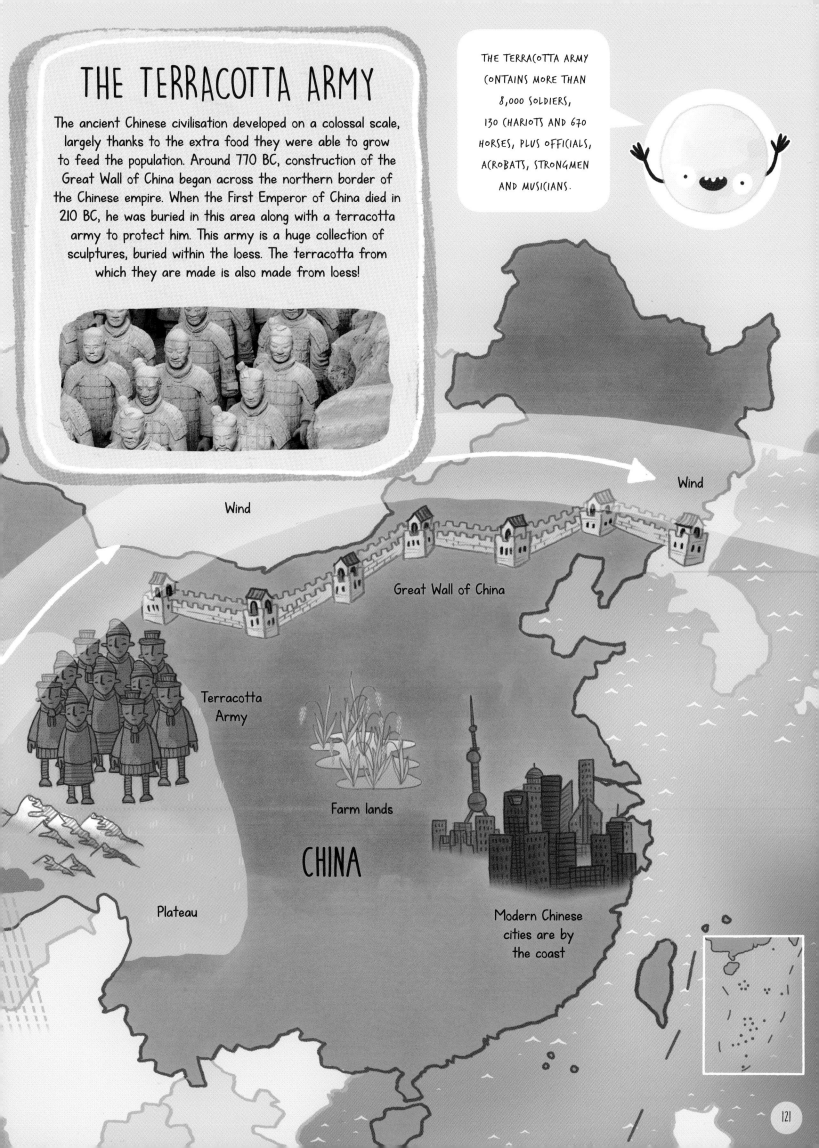

THE TERRACOTTA ARMY CONTAINS MORE THAN 8,000 SOLDIERS, 130 CHARIOTS AND 670 HORSES, PLUS OFFICIALS, ACROBATS, STRONGMEN AND MUSICIANS.

Wind

Wind

Great Wall of China

Terracotta Army

Farm lands

CHINA

Plateau

Modern Chinese cities are by the coast

DESERT WINDS

No continent on our planet has been more influenced by the wind than Australia. The centre of this huge country is known as the outback, and large parts of it are desert. There are no cities here and very few settlements of people as the landscape is too barren (meaning poor quality) for farming. This is because the winds strip away the nutrients from the land. In fact, film-makers often use the outback of Australia for films about Mars!

Although living in the outback is tough, some animals make it their home.

THE OUTBACK COVERS ALL OF INLAND AUSTRALIA, AND MOST OF NORTH AND NORTHWEST AUSTRALIA, SPANNING SEVERAL MILLION SQUARE KILOMETRES.

RED EARTH

Much of the soil in Australia's outback is red. This is because the soil contains iron, so the oxygen in the air turns it a rusty colour. The outback is also amazingly dusty. The soil is scorched by the intense heat from the Sun and very dry. All these factors mean large-scale crop farming can't happen here.

Brown snake

DESERT PAVEMENT

Sitting over central Australia is an enormous circular wind pattern, thousands of metres above the ground. The winds have been swirling in a great spiral around the continent, stripping away fertile soil, for hundreds of thousands of years. In China, fertile soil is carried in by the wind. But in the Australian outback, fertile dust and nutrients are simply blown away, leaving sand and stones behind. The landscape that is created is known as a 'desert pavement'.

DUST STORMS

Huge dust storms pick up the soil in the outback and, if the wind is strong enough, blow it all the way to the cities like Sydney in eastern Australia. In 2002, a record storm was more than 2,000 km (1,200 mi) long, and shifted almost 4.5 million tonnes of dust. Most of the dust ends up in the ocean, where it creates huge algal blooms. Algae is a water plant and the impact of extra nutrients from the dust hitting the water makes it grow rapidly.

Thorny devil

Desert bilby

HUMANS ADAPT

The climate and the winds were not kind to the people who first settled in Australia (see pages 58–59). The continent was barren and dry, so it made sense for people to live separately in small groups, following a hunter-gatherer lifestyle and foraging for wild plants than to farm. In parts of the world with fertile soil, powerful ancient civilisations developed because farming brought people together to form large groups.

123

TRADE WINDS

The winds that blow around our planet are grouped into flows called easterlies and westerlies - turn to pages 112-113 to read more about this. Around 500 years ago, humans realised they could use these winds to their advantage. Europeans wanted to explore more of the world and so they set sail. They noticed that if they left the southwest coast of Europe or Africa, the winds usually blew them away from the coast, in a south-westerly direction. This made it difficult to sail in the opposite direction, so rather than fight the wind, they used it to sail from east to west!

THE RETURN TRIP

European sailors who reached the Americas found that the return trip was a little trickier. If they sailed east, they got caught up in the same south-westerly trade winds that brought them to the Caribbean in the first place. Instead, they headed north along the American coast, and eventually picked up a wind that blew steadily from west to east - what we now know as a westerly. This blew them all the way back across the Atlantic Ocean.

Britain

Spa[in]

Atlantic
Ocean

Caribbean

Pacific
Ocean

MEANING BEHIND THE NAME

The winds that blew these explorers from east to west were named the 'trade winds'. The word 'trade' meant 'path' in the English language of the time, and the flow of these easterly winds was the pathway that sailors took when sailing across the Atlantic Ocean. By the 18th century, the trade winds were so important in the trading of goods between foreign nations that the word 'trade' became associated with this business. And this is what the word means today in English!

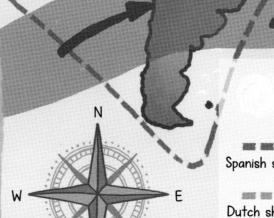

N

W   E

S

 Hurricanes, cyclones, typhoons

 Trade winds (south-easterly)

- - Spanish ships

Trade winds (north-easterly)

- - Dutch ships

Westerly winds

- - British ships

CONNECTED BY THE WIND

The trade route back and forth across the Atlantic Ocean was used to transport crops like sugar cane from the Caribbean to Europe, but it was also used to ship slaves from Africa to the Caribbean islands. Sugar cane plantation owners needed people to farm their crops, and so slaves were captured and sent from Africa to meet the demand, until slavery was abolished in the 19th century. Other cultures became connected due to the trade winds. The Dutch sailed to Indonesia by heading down Africa and then picking up the westerly winds. The Spanish traded with the Philippines with help from the easterlies. Groups who would previously not have interacted with each other were linked by the wind.

The therlands

Pacific Ocean

The Philippines

Indonesia

Indian Ocean

HURRICANES, CYCLONES AND TYPHOONS

Violent winds, heavy rain and thunderstorms – when weather like this hits, it is called a hurricane, cyclone or typhoon depending where in the world you are. In the Atlantic and northeast Pacific regions, a mega-storm is called a hurricane. In the northwest Pacific it is called a typhoon, and in the South Pacific and Indian Ocean it is called a cyclone. The flow of the trade winds affects the direction in which these huge storms travel. This means places like the Caribbean, the east coast of Africa, Southeast Asia and the northeast coast of Australia receive the majority of these storms.

PLAYING WITH THE WIND

Hang-gliding

Why is it that we often wish we could soar through the air like a superhero? It's probably because since ancient times humans have dreamt of spreading their arms and flying like a bird! We read on pages 88-89 about how inventors such as Leonardo da Vinci first began to devise flying machines. And of course now we can fly easily by simply hopping on a plane. But some people still look for that more authentic flying experience as this is how they can really have fun with the wind!

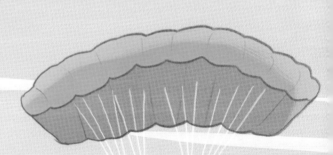

Parachuting

Sailing

Kitesurfing

Kite flying

KITESURFING

We know the force of uplift works on wings, but it also works on kites, sails, boards, wind turbines and more. That's because lift works in any direction. Take kitesurfing for example – the force of uplift works on a sail, which is attached to a board pulling the sail down. The kitesurfer balances the two forces to glide across the top of the waves. Using the force of the wind, kitesurfers can move at speed, do tricks and see for how long and how high they can jump off the waves!

A WINGSUIT WORKS USING LIFT, IN THE SAME WAY WE TALKED ABOUT ON PAGES 86-87. A TYPICAL SUIT IS WEBBED BETWEEN THE LEGS AND ARMS TO PROVIDE THE LIFT THE FLIER NEEDS.

THE WINGSUIT

The development of the wingsuit in the late 1990s means people can glide through the air just by wearing a special suit. Flying in a wingsuit is a mix of skydiving and gliding. Wingsuit wearers either jump from a plane or off a high mountain peak to get high enough height to make the wingsuit work. When they get close to the ground, they release a parachute and float back to Earth for a safe landing.

Skydiving in a wingsuit

RECORD WINDS

Scientists measuring the strongest winds on Earth found the windiest place to be Cape Farewell, in southern Greenland. Wind speeds often reach 20 m (65 ft) per second!

Parasailing

WIND POWER

Over the course of history, people have also looked at how they can harness the power of the wind and use it to their advantage. You may have seen wind turbines on a hill near where you live. The wind turns the blades to generate electricty which makes them one of the cleanest sources of renewable energy being used today. Denmark gets 40% of its electricity from wind! But did you know that humans have harnessed wind energy for 2,000 years or more? This is in the form of windmills where the wind turns blades which then generate a movement in the machine connected to them.

FIRE

The ancient Greeks believed that fire represented energy, force and passion. Some of them also thought that fire was the most important of the elements. But fire hasn't been on our planet for as long as the other three elements – the conditions on Earth had to be just right before the first spark could appear. Since it lit up our planet, fire has often been seen as a symbol of progress and knowledge because of its power to bring about change and fuel human development. Even in the modern day, fire can be dangerous and wild and we must use it carefully. If we need a reminder of just how powerful it is, we need only look up into the sky at the fiery ball named the Sun to realise that fire rules in space as well as on Earth!

FLAME!

Fire has many similarities to the other three elements. We can feel fire, just as we can feel earth, air and water. Fire can also be carried from one place to another. But there is something very different about fire. Earth, air and water are all types of matter that exist on their own - they're all made up of tiny particles called **atoms**, joined together. But fire isn't matter - fire is energy released when matter changes from one form to another as it burns and produces flames. Fire can only happen when there is material to burn.

CHEMICAL REACTIONS

Fire on planet Earth comes from a chemical reaction between oxygen in the air and a fuel, like wood. For a fuel to catch fire, there has to be enough heat for it to burn.

When wood gets hot enough, it changes chemically and gives off gases and small particles of carbon. We see the particles as smoke, which float in the air.

The chemical reaction also creates the heat that keeps the fire burning. And as the fuel heats up, it produces light, which we see as flames.

NO FIRE WITHOUT FLAMES

What springs to mind when you first think of fire? It could be the heat, or it could be the yellow-orange glow. More often than not, it's the flames, flickering out from the centre of the fire, like tongues of light. You can never guess where they'll end up next - they look so random and unpredictable.

FLAME COLOUR

Flames can be all sorts of different colours. We are used to seeing flames as orange, or maybe yellow, but the colour depends on what you're burning, and how hot it is. If you see different colours in a flame, that's because there's an uneven temperature within the fire.

The cooler parts of the flame glow yellow or orange at the tip.

The hottest part of the flame glows blue at the base.

DOWN ON PLANET EARTH, GRAVITY MAKES SURE THAT FLAMES BURN UPWARDS. THE HEAVY AIR IS PULLED DOWNWARDS AND LIGHT GASES IN THE FLAME FLOAT UPWARDS. IN SPACE, WHERE THERE IS NO GRAVITY, A FLAME WOULD BE SPHERICAL!

BEFORE FIRE

Let's start at the very beginning of our planet's life. Earth was created around 4.6 billion years ago. That's 4,600 million years or, to really spell it out, 4,600,000,000 years. It slowly formed out of tiny particles, all of which were swarming around the fiery new Sun in our Solar System (see pages 10-11). Over time, these tiny particles gathered together to become liquid and solid. Some particles cooled and formed the seas, while others became solid land. At the centre of planet Earth, the core raged with a fierce, fiery heat that meant the planet was alive and could evolve.

THE CREATION OF FIRE ON EARTH

4,600 mya, the earliest form of planet Earth was created.

For 90% of Earth's history, there was no fire. Earth was a barren planet of dust and rock and there was not enough oxygen in the air to allow burning.

4,400 mya, the Earth had cooled enough for liquid water to appear.

2,450 mya, the Great Oxygenation Event happened. Oxygen appeared in the air for the first time, given off by bacteria.

About 470 mya, fossil records show us that land-based plants appeared on Earth. Through the process of photosynthesis (see page 159), they pumped lots of oxygen into the air.

Over time, the rotted remains of plants were buried under soil and rocks and became fossils and fuel such as coal. You can read more about this on pages 156-159.

When oxygen levels on Earth reached a certain level (about 13%) around 420 mya, it meant fire could start. Dry plants burned when sparked by lightning or volcanic action, by reacting with oxygen.

Around 6-7 mya, grass grew for the first time in many areas on Earth. Grass burns very easily when it's dry and dead, which helped fire to spread.

Our human ancestors appeared 2.5 mya and so our relationship with fire began. Read on to find out more...

RECIPE FOR FIRE

Sit up and pay attention, it's time for a science lesson! When you think about it, a chemical experiment is like a recipe - you take the ingredients and make something new. And this is what we need to make fire. This particular recipe is a chemistry recipe, because that's what fire actually is - one of the products of a chemical reaction. Fire has three basic ingredients: fuel, oxygen and heat. You need all three ingredients in the recipe to make fire start. Luckily, if you understand how to make fire, you will also have a good idea of how to stop it!

INGREDIENTS FOR FIRE

1. Oxygen: this is easy enough to source, as nature provides it! There's oxygen in the air we breathe.

2. Fuel: you could use a number of different fuel sources, but let's stick to the fuel our ancestors first used, wood.

3. Kindling: this is a dried out version of our fuel, with a low water content, so it burns more easily and will get the fire going.

4. A spark: you need this to set the fire off in the first place.

5. Combustion: this is the chemical reaction needed to keep the fire going.

1. PREPARE THE SITE

Pick a site for your fire and a material you can use as fuel. We've chosen wood for our recipe, but nature uses anything that will actually burn, and which contains carbon.

2. LAY THE KINDLING

Kindling is the material used for lighting fires. It is often a very dry version of the main fuel and burns easily which creates the perfect conditions for the main source of fuel to ignite and keep burning.

THE MYTH OF THE PHOENIX

The phoenix, a bird from Greek mythology, is a creature that is linked to fire. It is made of flames and is born out of the ashes of a dying fire. Like a real fire, its life can be restarted again and again because an old fire can always be reborn. Simply add more fuel and a spark from the old fire will do the rest. The phoenix appears in many popular stories throughout history – you may have come across Fawkes in the Harry Potter series!

3. IGNITE THE SPARK

A spark is a hot, glowing particle that gets a fire going. The spark provides the heat to combine the chemicals in the fuel with the oxygen in the air. Sparks can be made by nature, such as volcanoes or lightning, or by rubbing sticks together to create friction. Today, people also use matches – but don't do this unless an adult is present!

4. COMBUSTION

This is the reaction between the fuel and the oxygen in the air, which allows the fire to flame. Beware – if you remove either the fuel, the oxygen or the combustion (i.e. the heat), the fire will stop.

THE NEED FOR FIRE

Imagine living a million years ago. Life was hard for our ancestors – nature was fierce and seemingly untameable. Their whole lives were spent struggling to stay alive. If it wasn't the dangerous predators stalking them at night, it was the constant search for food during the day. Where would the next meal come from? The potential power of fire for humans was huge. Fire could ward off life-threatening creatures, it could smoke out nasty biting insects, and fire could also cook food which could be kept for longer, so there was more to eat. Early people saw that flames were created by lightning, forest fire and even volcanoes, but they had to learn how to catch and control them.

EVIDENCE OF FIRE

The creation of fire by humans was one of the main turning points in our history, but scientists can't be sure exactly when this first happened. When we find ancient evidence of fire, how can we tell if it was made by lightning, a volcano or by human hand? Even when fire seems to have been started by humans – an old campfire in a cave, for example – how do we know if the fire was made from scratch, or just taken into the cave from a natural fire and kept alive for as long as possible?

CATCHING FIRE

Our prehistoric ancestors probably first captured fire by grabbing a burning stick from a wildfire and fanning the flames to keep it alight. Most scientists agree that humans had learnt to control fire around 125,000 years ago. But even earlier evidence of the control of fire ranges from 200,000 to 1.7 million years ago!

THE WORLD CATCHES FIRE

There's evidence of the early use of fire all around the world.

In Beeches Pit, Suffolk, England, there are signs of fire use from 415,000 years ago.

In Africa there are signs of fire at the Kalambo Falls, Zambia, where scientists found charred logs from about 110,000 years ago.

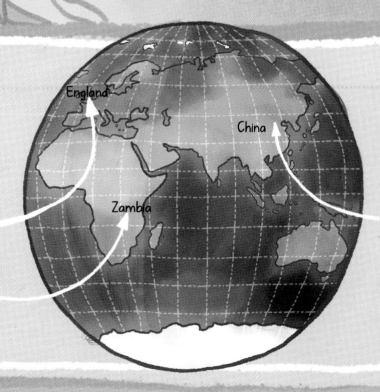

England

China

Zambia

In the Zhoukoudian Caves in China there is evidence of fire from as early as 230,000 to 460,000 years ago. These signs are from burnt bones, burnt chipped-stone artefacts, charcoal, and ash – all of which were found alongside fossils that can be dated.

FIRE AND FOOD

Our ancestors were very brave when they first captured fire as it is wild and unpredictable. Depending on where they lived it was also likely to be quite rare so they must have ventured close to the vent of volcanoes, or gone searching for a wildfire. Our ancestors must have planned to capture fire after they understood its power. We know from ancient myths and legends that humans knew all about the danger of fire, but also its benefits. Once they'd tamed the flames, humans first used fire for warmth and protection, and eventually for cooking.

HOT WATER

Finding hot, fresh water in nature is very rare. At first, humans learnt to heat water in leather buckets by dropping hot stones inside. Later, they found that if you coated a basket with thick clay, it could be put on a fire and the water within it would boil without cracking the pot.

SOMETHING'S COOKING

Cooking first started when people started the custom of sitting around a fire for warmth and light. From here they learnt that they could roast a piece of meat by holding it over the fire on a stick.

COOKING UP CHEMISTRY

Humans first came across chemistry through cooking! They noticed that clay pots could hold liquids, which could be heated over a fire. They started to notice the changes in the pot's contents. The liquid changed consistency, or evaporated entirely into a gas. By witnessing this process people realised that materials could change from one state to another.

THE USE OF FIRE AND THE NEED FOR FOOD ALSO HELPED HUMANS UNDERSTAND BIOLOGY. TO MAKE SURE THEY WEREN'T POISONED, EARLY HUMANS HAD TO BE SURE ABOUT THE PROPERTIES OF PLANTS AND HOW THEY CHANGED WHEN COOKED.

A COOKING CHEMISTRY EGG—XAMPLE

A good example of fire and heat being the basis of chemistry is eggs! Think about what happens when you boil an egg. It starts off all gloopy and fluid but, after heating, it ends up all squidgy and solid – especially if you hard-boil it. The gloopy-to-squidgy change is a chemical reaction in the egg as a result of heat.

FIRE AND HUMANS

Fire lit up the history of early humans. Just think about all the important developments that started with fire – light, warmth, cooking. We know how important fire was to our ancestors as they recorded it in their incredible cave art. But think about it, even this art would have been impossible without fire, as the artists would not have been able to see in the dark caves!

THE EVOLUTION OF HUMANS WITH THE HELP OF FIRE!

Fire created things that we take for granted nowadays. But thousands of years ago, simple things like light at night gave humans greater control over their lives. As our early ancestors learnt how to tame nature, they could make their own impact on the world.

Controlling fire meant our earliest ancestors could stay up at night as they had light. Those scary animals in the dark and biting bugs don't like fire and smoke so fire provided safety as well.

Over time, early humans began to lose much of their thick body hair. Warm fire meant that humans coped better with the cold as it generated heat for them.

Fire helped our ancestors to become better hunters. They used fire to melt 'pitch' which created a glue that could be used to attach flint points onto the ends of wooden spears. And heat could be used to harden spear points.

MODERN HUMANS

Fire helped set our human ancestors on the journey to becoming modern humans. Over hundreds of thousands of years, healthier, smarter humans have had the time, the brain power and the materials to invent all of the items that we use in our modern lives.

Cooking food made humans healthier, too. Some plants are indigestible when they are raw, but when cooked their nutrients are unlocked and are absorbed much faster by the body.

Eating cooked food gave early humans more energy. This helped them to grow bigger brains over time. And bigger brains allowed humans to create primitive art using charcoal from burnt wood.

As our ancestors became more intelligent, they began to explore more distant and colder places. Over time, this meant humans spread out and gradually inhabited most areas of the planet.

HISTORY OF FIRE

Over thousands of years, our brave ancestors learnt how to capture and create fire. But being able to create your own fire doesn't mean you can always control it. There have been some major fire events which remind us of fire's great power.

AD 6
THE FIRST FIREFIGHTERS, ITALY

The earliest known firefighters, and the first fire brigade, were established in the city of Rome. A group known as the 'Vigiles' were instructed to protect Rome after fire damaged the city. They grew into a fire brigade of 7,000 people armed with axes and water buckets.

1871
THE GREAT CHICAGO FIRE, USA

In 1871 a fire in Chicago killed close to 300 people and left 100,000 homeless. Firefighters thought the fire would stop when it reached the river as the water would act as a natural firebreak. But along the river were lumber yards and coal stores, all of which burned with such intensity that the other side of the river caught fire from the heat and flying debris.

AD 64
THE FIRE OF ROME, ITALY

When the fire of Rome began, the weather was windy, which helped fan the flames as they blazed along the narrow, twisting streets. The ramshackle wooden buildings caught fire easily. Of Rome's 14 districts, three were totally destroyed and only four escaped without damage. When the city was rebuilt, the streets were made wider, to stop fires spreading in the future.

1666
THE GREAT FIRE OF LONDON, UK

This enormous fire started when a baker forgot to cover his hot ashes and a spark escaped. The fire burned for four days in the narrow streets of London, and destroyed the homes of 70,000 of the city's 80,000 inhabitants.

LESSONS LEARNT

Each of these great fires taught people several difficult lessons. To fight fire, you have to have an organised firefighting force, such as the Vigiles in Rome. You need to think about the structure of your town – wooden buildings that are built close together help fire to spread. And beware of the sheer heat of fires: in Chicago, the fire was so hot that natural firebreaks, such as a river, didn't make a difference. Finally, it's important to realise that some fires are uncontrollable.

1212
LONDON BRIDGE BLAZE, UK

The medieval version of London Bridge had buildings running along its length. When a fire broke out at one end of the bridge, people rushed out of the buildings and into the middle of the bridge, intending to cross the river. But high winds quickly carried red-hot embers across the river and set fire to buildings at the other end, trapping the people in the middle.

1923
THE KANTO EARTHQUAKE, TOKYO, JAPAN

The Kanto earthquake struck at lunchtime, so many people were cooking food over open fires. As these fires became uncontrolled they joined together across the city to form firestorms so intense that they created their own wind system. Over 140,000 people died, many when their feet became stuck on the melting tar on the roads.

2009
BLACK SATURDAY BUSHFIRE, VICTORIA, AUSTRALIA

This was the deadliest bushfire event ever recorded in Australian history. High temperatures and strong winds spread the fire around the dry bush land in no time at all. Turn the page to read more about it.

WILDFIRE !

Early humans lived surrounded by the wildness of nature most of the time, and there was always a chance that it could turn into a fiery inferno at any minute. That's what the experience of wildfire must have seemed like to our ancestors – the entire world suddenly ablaze. Temperatures in wildfires can sometimes reach hundreds, if not thousands, of degrees. Wildfire is still a very real danger today, as people living in parts of Australia and America are well aware.

WHERE THE WILDFIRES ARE

Wildfires can be started by sparks from lightning or a volcanic eruption. But today, it's people that cause four out of every five wildfires. They start mainly in forested areas in countries that experience very high temperatures. Areas that are moist enough to grow trees, but also have long, dry, hot periods, are perfect locations for wildfire. Fires happen mostly in summer and autumn, when fallen branches and leaves dry out and become highly combustible.

THE LIFE OF A WILDFIRE

The fire begins during a **drought**. It starts not in the dense and humid trees, but among the grass and leaves, which are very dry and contain a lot less water.

BLACK SATURDAY FIRESTORM

Saturday 7th February, 2009, or Black Saturday, was the worst wildfire disaster in Australia's history. A week before the fires, a heatwave hit south-eastern Australia, with temperatures above 43°C (109°F) for three days running. On Black Saturday, hundreds of fires raged through the state of Victoria as many places recorded their hottest temperatures since 1859. The wildfires claimed the lives of 173 people, countless numbers of wildlife and destroyed almost 2,000 homes. Wildfires are devastating for wildlife as they destroy habitats and animals often can't escape the flames.

The wildfire front is where roaring flames meet the dry grass, leaves and wood. Even before a wildfire front arrives, the foliage dries out as the front warms the air to 800°C (1,470°F). This makes dry materials ignite faster and allows the fire to spread rapidly.

The wildfire front rips through the trees faster than a human can walk, and twice as fast through grassland. A fire can even jump! The wind carries hot wood embers, called firebrands, over roads, rivers and other firebreaks. This creates small fires as far as 20 km (12 mi) from the fire front.

As the wildfire gets larger, air rises as it is heated and powerful updrafts are created. These drafts draw in new, cooler air from the surroundings and the strong winds create fire whirls. The fire can spiral with tornado force speeds of more than 80 km/h (50 mph).

GREAT FIRE OF LONDON

Fires come in all shapes and sizes, from the firestorms of wildfires to small fires in fireplaces at home. Just as a wildfire in a forest can start from a spark and wipe out natural habitats, a fire in a city can begin indoors and escalate quickly to destroy a city. People learn from experience and so incidents like the Great Fire of London must be remembered to avoid history being repeated.

SAMUEL PEPYS RECORDED THE EVENTS OF THE FIRE IN HIS DIARY

Sunday 2nd September, 1666

1am: A fire breaks out at the bakery of Thomas Farriner, on Pudding Lane.

3am: The maid of Samuel Pepys, famous diary-writer of the time, wakes him to tell him about the fire.

7am: Pepys is told that 300 houses have already been destroyed.

7am: The water-house over the tower at St Magnus' church is burnt, stopping the water supply and harming efforts to fight the fire.

8am: Fishmongers' Hall burns down, the first of 44 company halls to be destroyed.

9am: Laurence Pountney Church bursts into flames, ignited by flying sparks.

10am: Pepys travels to tell King Charles II to command the Lord Mayor to pull down houses to make firebreaks.

12pm: Pepys meets the Lord Mayor and gives him the king's orders. The mayor replies: "I have been pulling down houses. But the fire overtakes us faster than we can do it."

3pm: Fierce fires burn in the riverside warehouses, fed by flammable goods inside – wine, oil, tar, coal and timber.

Monday 3rd September, 1666

8am: King Charles II and the Duke of York take command of the fire-fighting, and have 'fire posts' set up, manned with 100 civilians and 30 foot soldiers.

THE END AND THE AFTERMATH

The fire ended partly due to good luck. The winds that were helping the fire to spread, simply died down. The Tower of London guards also used gunpowder to make firebreaks, which stopped the fire spreading east. Although the fire had a devastating effect, it also did some good as it wiped out the rats carrying the bubonic plague, a deadly disease which had infected Londoners the year before.

9am: People start to flee London, most going north and east.

10am: The fire approaches Cornhill and the Royal Exchange. Citizens pull down buildings to make a firebreak, but they forget to remove the rubbish from the street. The rubbish catches fire, and the buildings begin to blaze.

3pm: More fire posts are set up, as around 23 churches across London are burning at the same time.

Tuesday 4th September, 1666

5am: King Charles II and the Duke of York ride around the city, carrying over 100 guineas, which is given to workmen as a reward for their hard work.

8pm: St Paul's Cathedral catches fire. The cathedral's wooden scaffolding had been used to store people's belongings, as they thought the stone cathedral would not catch fire.

Wednesday 5th September, 1666

7am: Samuel Pepys climbs Allhallows tower and reports the fire has spread as far as the eye can see.

Thursday 6th September, 1666

Pepys is told about an isolated fire in Bishopsgate. It's the last outbreak of fire. More than 200 soldiers are brought in to clear the streets and dampen down the fire.

Friday 7th September, 1666

Samuel Pepys wakes to find 'all well'. King Charles II withdraws all troops brought in to fight the fire.

COOKING WITH FIRE

Remember how people first cooked food, by heating water in pots and placing meat on a stick over an open fire (see page 138)? Since those primitive cooking methods, two important things have happened. Firstly, humans have brought fire indoors after thousands of years of cooking outdoors. Secondly, we've learnt how fire works and how hot it can get. With this knowledge, we have created different kinds of ovens, which use the heat and flames from a fire in various ways.

THE BRICK OVEN

The Egyptians and Romans, and other ancient cultures, used stone or brick ovens to bake bread. A wood fire was lit inside a dome made of brick and the heat from the fire was contained within. This early design hasn't changed very much, as big brick ovens are still the best way to cook crispy wood-fired pizza today!

THE BEEHIVE OVEN

In the 16th and early 17th centuries in America, people built brick ovens shaped like beehives. Bakers burnt what they thought was the right amount of wood into ash in these brick ovens. Then, they stuck their hand in the oven to test the temperature of the fire (do not try this at home!). If it was too hot, they opened the door for a little bit; too cold and they added more wood.

GAS OVEN

The first use of gas as a flame for cooking was recorded in 1802, by Zachaus Winzler from Moravia, which is now in the Czech Republic. By 1834, gas stoves were on sale to the public. Customers quickly caught on that gas stoves were easier to use and maintain than wood or coal stoves.

CAST IRON STOVE

This 1795 invention by Count Rumford, an American-born British scientist, used a single fire source to cook several pots at the same time at different temperatures. Not only that, but the heat from the stove also warmed the room.

THE WOK AND THE STIR FRY

Until the 16th century, Chinese cooking was known for its tasty stews. But stews take a long time to cook and plenty of wood is needed to keep the fire going. When wood became scarce, a new, quicker cooking method was needed that used less fuel. The Chinese came up with a brilliant gadget, which is known across the globe today as the wok! Intense heat from a flame is focused at the base of the wok and this area can cook food quickly. The curved sides mean the entire wok also heats up so it can cook a lot of ingredients in one go.

ELECTRIC OVEN

At the end of the 1800s, once electricity had arrived in people's homes, cooking with electricity wasn't far behind. Flames do a disappearing act in these electric stoves which are used in many homes today.

GUNPOWDER AND FIREWORKS

Isn't a firework a perfect symbol for fire? It's beautiful to look at, but it's also very dangerous! Around the 7th century AD, the Chinese discovered, probably accidentally, that mixing gunpowder with sulphur and charcoal caused a loud BANG! The firecracker quickly became a popular fixture at festivals as the noise was thought to scare away evil spirits. But bamboo firecrackers were also used by archers, who attached them to arrows and fired them at the enemy in battle.

GUNPOWDER INGREDIENTS

Gunpowder is a mixture of three things that the Chinese have known about since ancient times: charcoal, sulphur and saltpetre (which is potassium nitrate, a white powdery mineral which makes hot coals burn more fiercely by providing extra oxygen). If you get the mixture of these three things just right, gunpowder burns strongly and throws out fiery sparks – the basic firework.

A BURST OF COLOUR

It may have been the Chinese who invented the firework, but it was the Italians who gave fireworks all those amazing colours. In the 1830s scientists realised that different chemicals give off different colours when they burn. For example, lithium is red, sodium fires yellow and copper burns blue.

FIREWORKS AND THE FIRST ASTRONAUT

In the 16th century, long before the days of NASA, there lived a man named Wan-Hu. According to legend, this minor Chinese official of the Ming Dynasty tried to launch himself into space!

Wan-Hu's spacecraft was a large wicker chair, with 47 bamboo tubes, packed with gunpowder, attached to the frame. What could go wrong?

He called 47 assistants, each armed with a flaming torch, and told them to rush forward and set fire to the long fuses. There was a tremendous fiery roar and huge explosion.

When the smoke cleared, the rocket chair was gone and Wan-Hu had disappeared and was never seen again. It's unlikely he made it to the Moon but he has left a trace because the Russians named a crater after him.

THE STEAM ENGINE

"I sell here, Sir, what all the world desires to have – power!" These words, from the year 1776, belong to Matthew Boulton, the man whose money paid for improvements to the steam engine. The engine works by using fire to heat water and create steam, which then builds in pressure and is used to move pistons to drive machines. The steam engine set us on a path to an industrial way of life. Over the next two centuries, steam power was harnessed to drive ships, cars and trains, and to power machines in factories.

HOW IT WORKS

A typical locomotive steam engine consists of a firebox, a boiler, a steam pipe and a chimney. The source of the engine's power is its firebox as this part is where the fuel is burnt. The heat from the fire warms up the water in the boiler so that it comes out as super-heated steam. The steam coming out of the boiler then applies a force to a piston, which is used to turn the locomotive's wheels. Simple, really!

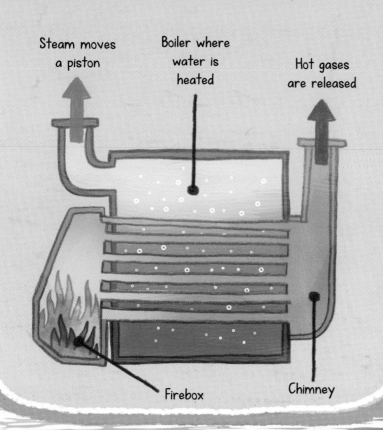

Steam moves a piston

Boiler where water is heated

Hot gases are released

Firebox

Chimney

CHOO–CHOO!

Some of the steam created by a steam engine is forced into the engine to move a piston, and some steam is released into the air as exhaust steam. This is why steam trains have to take on water at railway stations: they need to top up the water in the boiler that is constantly being lost through the steam exhaust. This also explains the choo-choo sound. The train driver opens a valve to release the steam exhaust through a whistle. The steam escapes under tremendous pressure and makes a 'choo' sound as it does!

A NEW INVENTION

It was the human thirst for fire-power that led to the creation of the steam engine. In 1712, Thomas Newcomen installed his invention, a steam engine which could pump water from coal mines, in Devon in the UK. This allowed coal miners to dig deeper and extract more coal from underground. Many people consider Newcomen to be the Father of the Industrial Revolution. Read more about coal from page 156 onwards.

THE COMBUSTION ENGINE

Fire powers almost all modern cars, motorbikes, boats, aeroplanes, large ships and helicopters. But how? With the internal combustion engine. Have you ever looked under the bonnet of a car and wondered what's going on? There's certainly not a simple steam engine under there. Although the internal combustion engine of a car is quite simple. Its purpose is to convert fuel into motion so the car can move. The fuel is burnt inside the engine which is why it's called an 'internal' combustion engine.

A TALE OF TWO ENGINES

Once again, it was the human quest for fire-power that provided the spark of inspiration. After the creation of the steam engine, inventors were still looking for ways to improve on this. A steam engine is an 'external' combustion engine. The burning of fuel happens outside the engine and it's the steam that makes the motion. An internal combustion engine is more efficient because the fuel is inside the engine. Internal combustion engines also tend to be a lot smaller and much lighter which is why you don't see many steam-driven cars on the road today!

HOW IT WORKS

A tiny amount of fuel (such as gasoline) is put in a small, enclosed space. Next, the fuel is ignited by a fiery spark. A huge amount of energy is released by the explosion of the fuel in the form of expanding gas. That energy is used to create a cycle that sparks off mini explosions hundreds of times every minute, creating more and more energy. Bingo, you have the makings of that complex car engine! Almost all cars currently use what is called a four-stroke combustion cycle to convert fuel into motion. The four strokes (or steps) are:

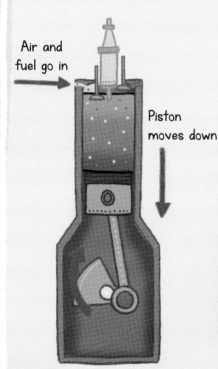

Air and fuel go in

Piston moves down

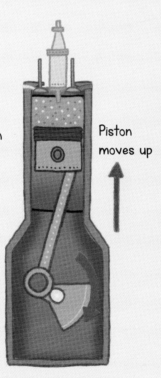

Piston moves up

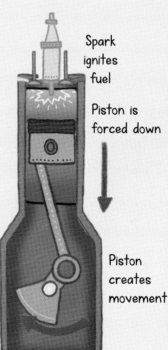

Spark ignites fuel

Piston is forced down

Piston creates movement

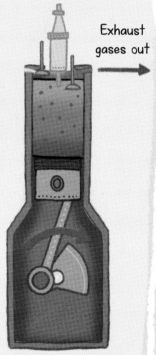

Exhaust gases out

1. Intake – piston moves down which allows the engine to take in air and fuel. Only the tiniest drop of fuel is needed.

2. Compression – piston moves up to compress the fuel/air mixture. Compression makes the explosion more powerful.

3. Explosion – fiery spark ignites the fuel and energy from the explosion drives the piston down. The movement is used to make the car go.

4. Exhaust – valve opens to let any exhaust materials out of the engine.

FOSSIL FUEL

The term fossil fuel generally means coal, gas and oil. They create fire when they burn, which creates energy. Each type of fuel has its own story, but they also have things in common. They've all been made from the fossilised remains of prehistoric plants and animals, which is why they are called **non-renewable** sources of energy, as they take millions of years to form. Read on through the next few pages to find out why these fuels have been so important to human development.

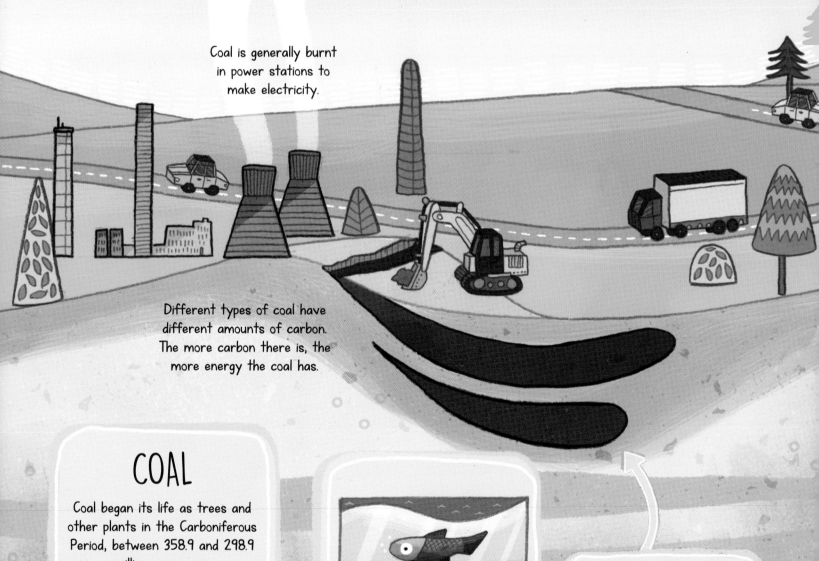

Coal is generally burnt in power stations to make electricity.

Different types of coal have different amounts of carbon. The more carbon there is, the more energy the coal has.

COAL

Coal began its life as trees and other plants in the Carboniferous Period, between 358.9 and 298.9 million years ago.

When plants and animals died they were buried under many layers of rocks, soil and water, and pressed down, deep underground.

The intense pressure and extreme heat underground turned these ancient plants into the hard, black, brittle rock called coal.

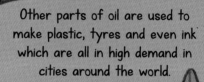

Oil has to be treated in refineries before it can be used, then it is cleaned and separated into different kinds of fuel.

Other parts of oil are used to make plastic, tyres and even ink which are all in high demand in cities around the world.

The most important fuel we get from oil is petrol, used for powering boats, cars and planes.

Gas can be used in its raw form. Perhaps you have it in your house for heating and cooking?

OIL AND GAS

Natural gas and oil are made from the remains of tiny sea creatures and plants that lived millions of years ago – long before dinosaurs roamed the Earth.

When these creatures died and were buried, the immense pressure created gas, which became trapped under layers of rock in the Earth's crust, like water in a sponge.

Oil formed when the remains of the sea creatures were exposed to high heat and pressure. The liquid was trapped under layers of rock.

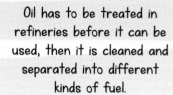

COAL AS FROZEN ENERGY

Coal, one of the three fossil fuels, is an incredible material – it used to be called 'black diamond' because of its high value to people. Throughout history, coal taken from the ground has provided power for humans. But where exactly does its high energy store come from?

CARBONIFEROUS PERIOD

We know that coal is made from plants, but the reason we have so much of this fossil fuel is because during the Carboniferous Period, 359–299 mya, most of planet Earth was covered in swamps and forests. Trees grew tall quickly in the warm, oxygen-rich climate of the time and as soon as they died they were rapidly buried under new plant-life. It is these layers upon layers of Carboniferous plants that created the coal we use today.

Amphibians dominated the land in the Carboniferous Period and the first reptiles began to evolve.

Step 4. The chemical reaction creates a sugar, which plants use to grow, and oxygen which they release into the air.

PHOTOSYNTHESIS

The crucial factor in the creation of coal is a process called photosynthesis. 470 mya – way before the clammy Carboniferous Period – plants on Earth learnt how to absorb the Sun's energy in the form of sunlight. Plants use this solar energy to extract carbon from the carbon dioxide in the air, and then use this to grow. It is this carbon in plants that burns in a fire, releasing the energy that originally came from the Sun's light.

Step 3. Plants use the energy from the sunlight to create a chemical reaction between the water and the carbon dioxide.

Step 2. Plant leaves take in carbon dioxide from the air and energy from sunlight.

Ingredients for photosynthesis: water from the ground, energy from sunlight and carbon dioxide from the air.

During the Carboniferous Period, Earth had the highest levels of oxygen in the air due to all the plants releasing it as a product of photosynthesis. The air was 35% oxygen compared to 21% today.

Step 1. Water is taken up from the ground by the roots of plants.

FROZEN IN TIME

As the great plants of the Carboniferous Period died and were buried deep in the earth, they gradually turned into coal and their energy became frozen in time. Because of photosynthesis, these layers of coal have preserved the Sun's energy from millions of years ago. When we burn coal today, the flame you see is actually the Sun's energy set free again. Coal is frozen sunlight!

MASTERY OF METAL

The history of human existence on Earth is often talked about in terms of the materials people used at particular points in time, for example the Bronze Age and Iron Age. But most metals, apart from gold and tiny amounts of copper, are not found in their raw state, they have to be melted out of the rocks in which they're found. So how did people discover these history-making metals? A form of carbon – charcoal – played an important role. Charcoal is partly-burnt wood and its use in making metals is the first stage in the story of how humans discovered fossil fuels.

CHARCOAL

Ancient people used charcoal for fires because it burns slower, hotter and with less smoke than wood. Charcoal, red and yellow ochre, and manganese oxide were used around 30,000 years ago to make some of the earliest cave paintings and rock art, such as this one in South Africa showing an ancient archer. But around 6,000 years ago there was a huge breakthrough with charcoal: as it burns at a scorching 1,100°C (2,000°F) it is hot enough to melt metal out of rock. The invention of metal smelting, which led to the discovery and use of iron, was one of the most critical turning points in human history.

THE AGES OF METAL

The Stone Age, the Bronze Age, the Iron Age – we have named periods in history after the technology and main material people used at the time. Fire played a key role in all three ages, but especially in the two metal ages. The word 'metal' comes from the Greek language, and means 'to search', which suggests that metal was scarce and people had to look hard for it. Metals were precious and only used for jewellery and ornaments, like this gold Bronze-Age necklace.

THE BRONZE AGE (BEGINS c.3000 BC)

Thanks to fire, people discovered how to make bronze, by melting and mixing copper with tin. This mixture of two metals is called an alloy. Bronze is much harder than copper on its own, and makes stronger weapons. People were able to carve wood for the first time with bronze tools, and so created the wooden wheel.

THE IRON AGE (BEGINS c.1200 BC)

The Iron Age began when people discovered how to heat and melt the iron out of ironstone rock, a process called smelting. Iron weapons became more widespread because iron was easier to find and work with than bronze. This allowed small groups of horsemen and seafarers to make stronger weapons, and eventually challenge the power of large Bronze Age ruling empires.

THE QUEST FOR COAL

Being able to extract metal from rock gave us tools, money and weapons – it was the basis of modern human progress. But we became victims of our own success. By the 16th century the use of charcoal for iron smelting was such a major industry that we began to run out of wood. In the growing cities in Europe and Asia, people looked for new sources of fuel for their fires.

ANCIENT WOODS

More than 3,000 years ago, Britain was covered by forests. Wood was a readily available fuel for people to burn on their fires.

DEFORESTATION

By the end of the 1500s, 90% of Britain's forests had been chopped down for fuel, to build homes or to clear land for growing crops. Around the globe, there was a similar story.

COAL TO THE RESCUE

Instead of burning carbon from the present in the form of charcoal made from wood, coal gave us carbon from the past. Coal wasn't readily available in all corners of Earth. So an element of luck played a crucial role in human history. The first place to benefit from the discovery of coal was Britain as it had lots of coal, lying just under the ground.

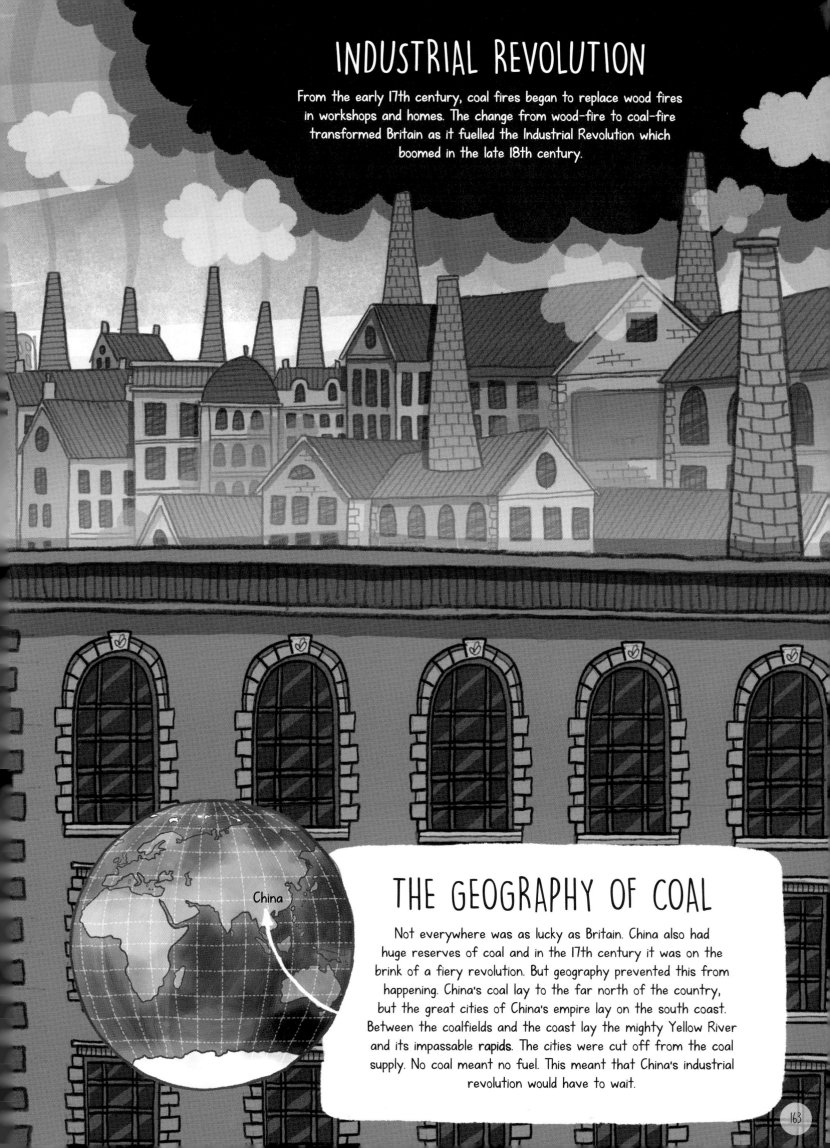

INDUSTRIAL REVOLUTION

From the early 17th century, coal fires began to replace wood fires in workshops and homes. The change from wood-fire to coal-fire transformed Britain as it fuelled the Industrial Revolution which boomed in the late 18th century.

China

THE GEOGRAPHY OF COAL

Not everywhere was as lucky as Britain. China also had huge reserves of coal and in the 17th century it was on the brink of a fiery revolution. But geography prevented this from happening. China's coal lay to the far north of the country, but the great cities of China's empire lay on the south coast. Between the coalfields and the coast lay the mighty Yellow River and its impassable rapids. The cities were cut off from the coal supply. No coal meant no fuel. This meant that China's industrial revolution would have to wait.

OIL ORIGINS

Most of the fossil fuel we use today comes from petroleum. This occurs naturally underground, and is better known as crude oil. Crude oil was made over millions of years from the remains of tiny plants and animals, called plankton, living in the sea. If the seabed is not disturbed, plankton will slowly transform into oil over about 150 million years. So the plankton that lived at the time of the dinosaurs became the crude oil we use today. When we burn it, we're seeing prehistoric fire!

1. LIFE IN THE SEA

The shallow seas of our planet are teeming with carbon-based life. Even today, there's more life in the top 3 m (10 ft) of the seas than in all of the Earth's atmosphere. When all these plants and sea-creatures die, their remains build up on the ocean floor.

2. LAYERS OF CARBON

Over millions of years, layer upon layer of dead sealife builds up on the ocean floor. From time to time, the seas evaporate, and layers of salt also build up. Slowly but surely the remains change into a carbon-rich gloop and become buried under rock.

THE ROLE OF THE SALTY SEA

Oil flows easily through many kinds of rock, like water through a sponge. This means that a great deal of the oil that was formed from the remains of sea creatures reached the Earth's surface long ago and has now disappeared. But in some parts of the world, thick layers of salt or dense rock trapped the oil, so it is still sitting there waiting for us to extract it today.

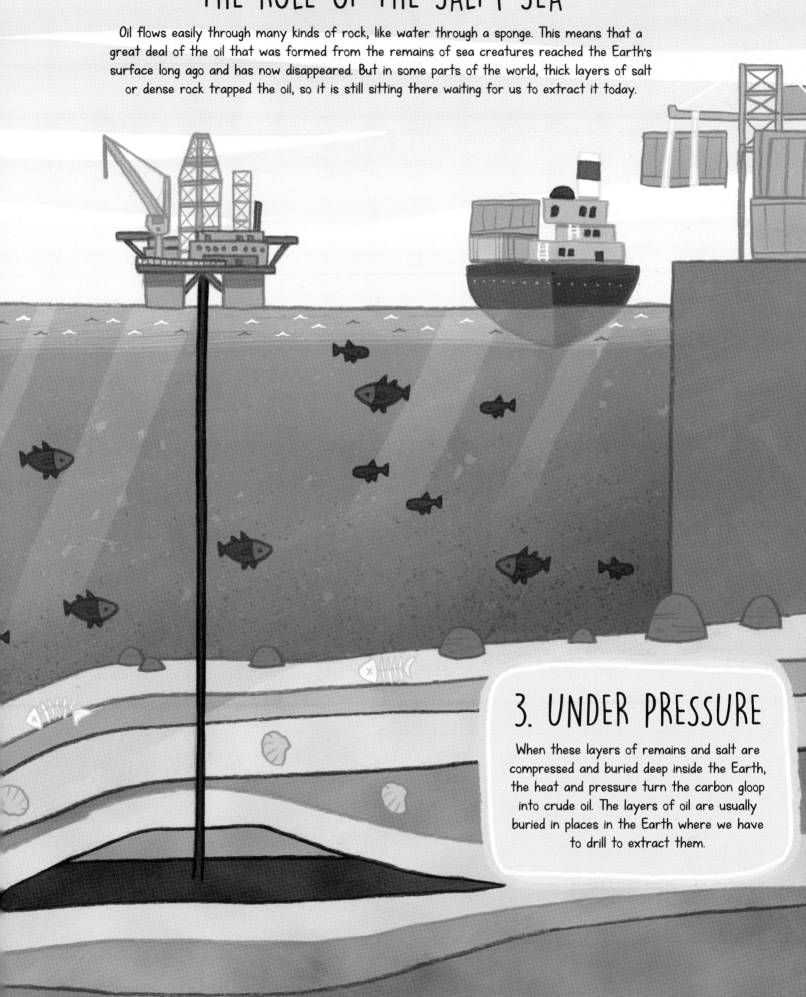

3. UNDER PRESSURE

When these layers of remains and salt are compressed and buried deep inside the Earth, the heat and pressure turn the carbon gloop into crude oil. The layers of oil are usually buried in places in the Earth where we have to drill to extract them.

OIL RUSH

The use of oil is another great example of how people have discovered new sources of fuel and mastered fire power. But finding the oil that has powered modern industry has been a huge adventure. We have to use cutting-edge science and technology because oil is often hard to find, and lies in remote places. Looking for oil is like detective work. Rock experts, known as geoscientists, look for important clues. And they have special tools to help them 'see' under the rocks and find crude oil.

THE VOLUME OF CRUDE OIL IS MEASURED IN BARRELS. ONE BARREL IS 159 LITRES (42 GALLONS). THE TERM DATES BACK TO THE 1860S WHEN THE OIL WAS ACTUALLY STORED IN WOODEN BARRELS.

DRILLING

The only way to be sure there's oil in the ground is to drill a well. This is tricky as not all wells lead to oil, and the cost of drilling an oil well is very expensive – it can cost up to £500 million ($630 million)! Geoscientists can save a lot of money by doing their detective work before drilling begins. Once oil is found, it can take from three to ten years to actually use it. This depends where the oil field is, and whether or not it lies deep below the bottom of the sea!

REFINING

Once oil starts flowing, it needs to be converted from crude oil and refined into the products we use in everyday life, such as car tyres, plastics and cosmetics. This is done in an oil refinery, which costs billions of pounds to build and run. A refinery uses heat to convert the crude oil into different parts, or 'fractions'. The oil evaporates into a vapour, and when it **condenses**, the fractions become liquid again at different temperatures.

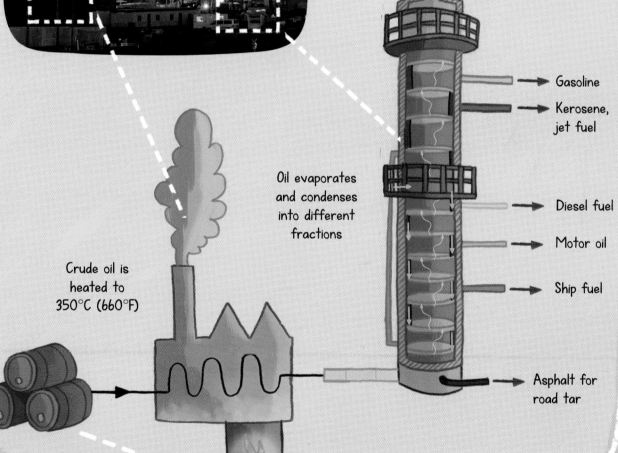

Gases out

Gasoline

Kerosene, jet fuel

Diesel fuel

Motor oil

Ship fuel

Asphalt for road tar

Oil evaporates and condenses into different fractions

Crude oil is heated to 350°C (660°F)

A WORLD RUN ON OIL

The world is fired by oil. It's the ultimate source of concentrated carbon energy. It is more energy-rich than coal, easier to transport and it has a million different uses. Crude oil plays a vital part in modern life. Oil powers our cars. We rely on oil for plastics, packaging, **pesticides**, fabrics for the clothes we wear and the electronics in our laptops and smartphones. Oil products are found in things as different as deodorant and nappies, footballs and car tyres, games consoles and MP3 players!

OIL-BASED PRODUCTS

OIL TIMELINE

3000 BC
The Mesopotamians used rock oil in building work as a kind of glue. They also used it in medicines.

2000 BC
The Chinese used crude oil for lighting and heating.

AD 300-400
The first oil wells were drilled in China using basic bamboo poles.

1907
Two big oil companies, Royal Dutch and Shell, merged to create one large company that rapidly expanded around the world.

1907
Oil was discovered in Iran, in the Middle East.

1920
By 1920 there were 9 million cars in the USA, and 'gas' stations opened everywhere selling petrol.

THE MONEY IN OIL

Oil has created enormous wealth. It's been used for thousands of years, but the oil industry only really fired up to full throttle just over 150 years ago. There were few places on the planet where it was easier to extract oil than Azerbaijan. Here, the oil just happened to be really close to the surface. The locals used it as a health remedy for thousands of years, but by the middle of the 19th century, the demand for oil rocketed. Entrepreneurs rushed to Azerbaijan to find their fortunes and the Shell oil company began life here. But all oil deposits come to an end eventually. Azerbaijan faded from fame, and the Middle East became the next key oil-producing region in the world.

1859

Edwin Drake started the modern oil industry when he discovered an oil **reservoir** only 21 m (69 ft) underground in Pennsylvania, USA.

1885

Karl Benz built the first internal combustion engine vehicle. It used liquid gasoline fuel.

1890s

The mass production of cars created a huge demand for gasoline.

1932

The first oil was discovered on the Arabian Peninsula, in Bahrain.

1954

The British Petroleum (BP) oil company was formed.

1950s onwards

With the growing use of cars and motor transport, oil became the most used energy source.

OIL SLICK

So much of today's world is powered by oil. But in order to use oil, it has to be delivered somewhere where you can buy it, such as a petrol station. Transporting crude oil from an oil well to a refinery, and getting oil products to customers is a big global business. Millions of barrels of oil are transported around the globe every single day via a huge network of pipelines, fleets of ships called oil tankers, and thousands of specialist trains. Great care is taken to avoid fires, explosions and spills. But sometimes accidents do happen and the consequences are huge, both for the environment and for wildlife.

OIL DISASTERS

1967

The oil tanker, *Torrey Canyon*, crashed into a reef in the sea, between the Isles of Scilly and the coast of Cornwall, UK. It was the world's worst oil spill at the time, and is still the UK's worst oil disaster to date. Around 35 million gallons of oil polluted 195 km (120 mi) of the Cornish coast.

1978

Another oil tanker, the *Amoco Cadiz*, lost its rudder in severe gales off the coast of England. The tanker was towed to France, but ran aground 5 km (3 mi) off the coast of Brittany, in the northwest of France. The tanker's entire cargo of 56 million gallons of crude oil spewed out along 160 km (100 mi) of the French coast. More than 20,000 birds died in the spill, and around 9,000 tons of oysters perished.

1991

The sister ship of the *Amoco Cadiz*, a tanker called *MT Haven*, exploded near Genoa, in Italy. The ship sank three days later, after breaking into two parts. Five crew members died in the disaster, and almost 12 million gallons of oil were spilt. The spill has been called the Mediterranean's worst environmental disaster.

1991

The worst oil disaster in history was actually deliberate. During the Gulf War, the retreating Iraqi army opened the valves at an oil terminal, draining oil into the Persian Gulf. Half a billion gallons of crude oil formed a slick, 10 cm (4 in) thick, covering 10,400 km^2 (4,000 sq mi).

2010

The Deepwater Horizon disaster happened when a drilling rig exploded in the Gulf of Mexico. Eleven workers were killed in an accident that kept a well gushing oil for 87 days. It's the largest marine oil accident in history, as 175 million gallons spewed out into the sea from Texas to Florida in the USA.

CLEVER CARBON

Oil and other fossil fuels, such as coal and natural gas, all have carbon as their main component. In fact, carbon can be found in every living thing on the planet. Human beings breathe in oxygen and breathe out carbon dioxide. Plants take in carbon dioxide to photosynthesise. Carbon also combines with hydrogen, oxygen and nitrogen to form life's complex chemicals, such as **proteins** and DNA. Because carbon is so versatile, it occurs everywhere on Earth and is always on the move. The carbon cycle shows how it moves around the planet.

Sunlight is needed for photosynthesis.

Carbon is absorbed by plants as carbon dioxide during the process of photosynthesis.

People and animals eat plants, taking in carbon.

THE CARBON CYCLE

Carbon passes from the air, into all living things, then to dead organic material, which is either eaten by decomposers (organisms that break down dead plants and animals) or becomes a fossil fuel. Then carbon passes back into the air as carbon dioxide. The cycle has many sources (things that add carbon to the air) and many sinks (things that remove carbon from the air). When there is too much carbon dioxide in the air, this creates an inbalance and causes global warming.

FEWER SINKS

An important sink in the carbon cycle are trees. They take in carbon dioxide from the air and use it in photosynthesis. But deforestation (see page 162) has reduced this sink which means there are fewer trees to take in the carbon dioxide from the air.

CARBON FOOTPRINT

When fossil fuels burn, they release carbon dioxide into the air. The amount of carbon dioxide released when fossil fuels are used is known as a 'carbon footprint'. You might have heard this phrase in relation to air travel or driving a car. The fuel used to transport you adds up to your carbon footprint. To help reduce the amount of carbon dioxide being released into the atmosphere and contributing to global warming, try to reduce your own carbon footprint. For short trips, why not walk instead of going by car? Eat locally-grown food so it doesn't have to be transported huge distances. Finally, turn off appliances such as televisions and computers when they're not being used, to reduce the amount of electricity needed from fossil fuel power stations.

There is carbon dioxide in the air.

Burning fossil fuels releases carbon dioxide into the air.

People and animals breathe out carbon dioxide.

CARBON DIOXIDE

Carbon dioxide is two oxygen atoms bonded to one carbon atom. You may see it written down as CO_2. It plays a big part in the carbon cycle as this is how carbon enters the air and the oceans – as a gas.

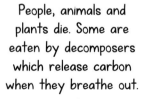

People, animals and plants die. Some are eaten by decomposers which release carbon when they breathe out.

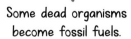

Some dead organisms become fossil fuels.

CARBON EVERYWHERE

Carbon's secret to success is that it is nature's best pattern maker. It can make long and strong chains with itself, linking up to form carbon-based substances like protein. Carbon can make patterns with other particles, allowing it to make materials as different as wood, fabric, diamonds and seashells!

Animals in the sea pass carbon into their shells. Over millions of years, shells turn into limestone rock. Weathering of the rock releases carbon dioxide into the air.

GLOBAL WARMING

Fossil fuels have been the engine of modern human history. They sparked the age of the machine and the Industrial Revolution. They spurred us on to create the steam engine and the internal combustion engine. Without them the modern world would look very different. But burning fossil fuels causes **pollution** and harms nature. And the biggest problem of all is global warming. Our planet is warming up, faster than at any time in Earth's history, and it's due to too much carbon dioxide being released into the atmosphere from burning fossil fuels.

WHAT IF WE DO NOTHING?

We've known since the 19th century that increased levels of carbon dioxide (CO_2) in the air raise the temperature on Earth. Burning fossil fuels means increased CO_2 levels. As temperatures rise, the ice caps start to melt, causing higher sea levels, flooding and loss of habitat for animals.

Global warming is making extreme weather events happen more often. There are more heavy rain downpours which cause flooding. There are also longer dry periods between the rainfalls, which, combined with higher temperatures, leads to drought.

The more we rely on fossil fuels, the more pollution we create. Oil spills happen when we transport crude oil around the world. Smog, soot and toxic air emissions are the result of burning coal. And acid rain happens when polluted air combines with water and falls as acidic rain.

THE FIRST FOSSIL FUEL BAN

King Edward I of England was a man ahead of his time. He tried to ban the use of coal in the year 1306! Wood had already become quite scarce so many metal workers and craftsmen turned to coal as a source of fuel for their fires. In some parts of England the air became dark and contaminated with thick coal smoke. The king worried it was beginning to poison the people so he imposed a ban on coal.

HOW CAN WE STOP GLOBAL WARMING?

Reduce, reuse and recycle! Recycling paper uses 65% less energy than making paper from raw materials. This means less fuel is required, so we could slow down manufacturing to a lower level.

To help reduce the negative effects of burning fossil fuels, we need to balance each source with a sink, for example by planting more trees. Research into this is vital as we haven't found the answer to balancing the amounts of carbon dioxide that are released against the amounts that are trapped.

Burning carbon is a huge world problem because it changes our climate. Renewable energy is the power of the future and we need to use energy sources from natural elements instead: geothermal (from the Earth), wind (from air), solar (from the Sun) and tidal (from water).

The Sun is the source of all life on Earth – it provides energy in the form of light and heat. It has enough fuel to power our entire Solar System for another five billion years and because light from the Sun is clean, and as good as endless, sunlight promises to be a free, renewable energy far into the distant future. It might sound like something from a sci-fi movie, but solar power is already with us! We use it to power things from pocket calculators to a NASA solar-powered plane.

SOLAR CELLS

Solar energy is energy from the Sun. Plants are clever enough to turn sunlight into food energy that they can store, but the human body can't do that! Nor can we use the Sun's energy directly to power a laptop, or a games console. But we have found a way of converting sunlight into other forms of energy, such as electricity.
Solar cells, or panels, are devices that catch sunlight and turn it into electricity. You might have seen them as dark, blue-black slabs on people's rooftops.

ENOUGH ENERGY TO POWER THE PLANET

Imagine flying around the globe, looking down upon the Earth as you soar high above. Sooner or later, all of the Earth's surface is drenched in beams of sunlight. Scientists say that, on average, every square metre (10 sq ft) of Earth's surface bathes in 164 joules (a unit of energy) of the Sun's energy per second, each day. That's enough sunlight to power a television! So think of this: if we could trap the energy from the Sun that falls on just 1% of the surface of the Sahara Desert, we could make enough electricity to power the whole world.

SOLAR FUTURE

All around the world, people are recognising the power of solar energy. Great solar farms are being built which use solar cells and solar panels in huge numbers to harness the Sun's energy. Solar power could generate as much as 27% of the world's electricity by 2050. And it's possible that solar energy could be our planet's largest source of electricity in the future.

SOLAR-POWERED POCKET CALCULATORS DON'T NEED BATTERIES. SOME DON'T EVEN HAVE AN 'OFF' BUTTON. THAT'S BECAUSE THEY WORK BY USING THE SUN'S POWER. THE TINY BLACK PANELS THAT SIT AT THE TOP OF THE CALCULATOR ARE THE SOLAR CELLS THAT CREATE THE POWER.

FIRE AS A SYMBOL

Why is fire such a strong symbol for humans? Imagine our early ancestors on a journey. As they travelled to new lands, they looked for the precious embers of dying fires. They kept those embers alive, and protected them from showers and downpours. Wherever people went, they carried fire with them which allowed them to move deeper into colder territory. You can see why fire is such an important symbol - humans have used fire every day for thousands of years. It's a symbol of human progress and civilisation.

FIRE AS A JOURNEY

Fire has illuminated our journey as we discovered the world. Its flame is a symbol for exploration and enlightenment. Fire has also powered human travel in the modern day. Without fire we wouldn't have invented complex engines. But we also use fire to fuel simpler forms of transport: to heat the air that allows hot-air balloons to rise, for example.

FIRE MEANS HOPE

An eternal flame is a fire that is made to burn continuously for a long period of time. Burning an eternal flame is a long-standing tradition in many cultures and religions. The flame symbolises events that people want to remember forever. For instance, the eternal flame in the Kremlin, a historic complex in the centre of Moscow, is kept alive to remember the 27 million Soviet citizens who died during World War II.

FIRE SYMBOLISES WISDOM

In ancient Greece, at the Temple of Delphi, there was a person known as an 'oracle'. The oracle was consulted on important decisions throughout the ancient world. Next to the oracle was an 'unquenchable fire'. It was thought that as long as the fire burned, the oracle's wisdom would remain.

FIRE REPRESENTS PAIN AND DEATH

The power of fire also means it is associated with pain and death, and has become a symbol for Hell. The idea of Heaven and Hell as places where good and evil people go when they die, comes from ancient Greek philosopher Plato, who lived between about 427 and 347 BC.

FIRE EQUALS ACHIEVEMENT

The Olympic flame is a symbol of the Olympic Games, the world's leading sporting event which takes place once every four years. Nowadays, the Olympic flame represents sporting achievement, but originally it represented the human theft of fire from the Greek God Zeus, by Prometheus. The Olympic flame is kept burning throughout the duration of the Games, and it burns eternally in Greece where the Games first began.

CAMPFIRES

In early human societies, campfires were the centre of the community. Fire provided warmth and light for all those living around the campsite. People used fires to cook their food. A campfire also served as a **beacon**, symbolising a human gathering for all those travellers who wished to join together and protect themselves against predators and insects.

STORYTELLING

From studying bushmen living today, scientists believe that campfires played an important role in developing human culture. During the day, talk around the fire was all about work. But at night-time, people gathered around a fire to sing and dance and share exciting stories. Storytelling around campfires may date back as far as 400,000 years. Our human ancestors would have shared their experiences of the day, and through story, tried to make sense of the world around them and their place in it.

ANCIENT CAMPFIRES

Evidence of charred antelope bones from caves in South Africa shows that early humans built campfires at least 1.6 million years ago. Some scientists believe that evidence of an ancient fire at the edge of the Kalahari Desert is the oldest known controlled fire. The fossils show that the materials in the fire were heated above 700°C (1,290°F) and from that we can tell that the fires burned with grasses and leaves. But scientists are not sure whether these early humans knew how to build campfires. Perhaps the flames were ignited by lightning and carried by hand to the mouth of the cave.

South Africa

LEOPARD'S STORY

An early campfire story tells of Leopard, Hyena and Jackal. They all hunted together until one day, Leopard was feeling unwell and wasn't strong enough to hunt. So, Leopard asked Jackal and Hyena if they could hunt some food for him. But both his friends made excuses and said they would not hunt for Leopard. "Fine," said Leopard, "if you won't hunt for me now, I will never share my food with you in future." Since that day, Leopard, and all leopards, have hidden their food in trees where their selfish friends can't reach it.

BEACONS OF LIGHT

Light cuts through the darkness of night-time, and that's why people have used fires as beacons of light for centuries. A beacon is a fire lit in a prominent place, on a mountain-top or large hill, to be used as a signal or to send a message. On land, beacons were used to warn groups that enemy troops were coming. At sea, they were used as lighthouses to warn sailors of hazards in the water.

The Byzantine Empire, AD 330-1453 used a beacon system to send messages across miles of countryside to the capital, Constantinople (which is modern day Istanbul). The system was designed by Leo the Mathematician, who was known as the cleverest man in Byzantium in the 9th century.

Ancient Romans lit fiery beacons to pass messages to each other. There's an account of the way they did this on the famous column of Trajan, in Rome.

The lighthouse of Alexandria, in Egypt, was one of the Seven Wonders of the Ancient World. Built around 80 BC a flame burnt at the top to direct ships safely around the coast at night.

The Vikings in Scandinavia had a network of beacons built on hill forts, to warn if there were any signs of robbers nearby.

In Wales, the mountains known as the 'Brecon Beacons' were so called because beacons were used to warn people living in the hills if the English were about to raid their villages.

The Great Wall of China was also a beacon network. Beacon fires along the wall were used to signal messages using smoke or fire.

Shipwreckers often made false beacons to look like lighthouses. They lit fires in places to direct ships away from safety and towards rocks. Once the ship sank, or ran aground, the shipwreckers stole the cargo and made money from the wreck.

FIRE WORSHIP

Fire is the only one of the four elements that humans can produce themselves. And that's one of the reasons why fire has been thought of as a bridge between people and their gods, or the Earth and sky. Many groups of people like to worship fire to give thanks for its presence in their lives. In some spiritual ceremonies, fire is considered an eternal flame. In others, fire represents the destruction of evil, rebirth and cleansing. The Navajo tribe are Native Americans who perform a Fire Dance every year, as part of their Mountain Chant ceremony. For them, it symbolises the defeat of evil.

THE MOUNTAIN CHANT EXPLAINED

The Navajo people have lived in southwest USA for thousands of years. Scientists say that the Navajo and their ancestors crossed the land bridge that connected Asia with Alaska, during the last Ice Age. But the Navajo believe otherwise and according to their history, they are descended from tribes that came from the south.

Navajo rituals represent the Earth and sky. Every year, towards the end of winter, they meet to mark the end of thunderstorms and to greet the new spring. The Chant is a healing ritual, not just for the sick, but for everyone, and is believed to restore balance to the natural world.

THE NAVAJO NATION

The Navajo are Native American people of the southwestern states of the USA, particularly Arizona, Utah and New Mexico. Every year in Arizona, to mark the end of winter, the Navajo perform a ceremony called the Mountain Chant which lasts for nine days. On the last day, a ceremony called the Fire Dance takes place.

The Chant is based on the legend of Dsilyi Neyani, the eldest son of a wandering Navajo family, who was captured by another tribe. It took him many years to find his family again, and he underwent many challenges along the way. These challenges are represented in the Mountain Chant. On the evening of the final day, a huge bonfire is lit. At dawn, when the embers are dying, the Fire Dance begins and dancers rekindle the fire, stoke it and dance. The dancers are covered in a white clay which protects them from the flames.

For the Navajo and other Native American tribes, fire is a symbol of destruction. The Fire Dancers expose themselves to intense heat to show that they are not afraid of fire, that they can control and defeat it, and thereby defeat evil. It is a cleansing ritual that the Navajo have practised for many thousands of years.

ALCHEMY

Fire is an incredible tool because it can change one substance into another. It can burn energy trapped in coal, and smelt metal from rocks. Fire can also easily destroy an entire forest – that's why our ancestors thought fire was so powerful, and believed that fire was the most important of the four elements. As far back as two thousand years ago, some people who were curious about what substances are made of developed alchemy to try and learn how to transform objects and to understand fire's power. Alchemy later developed into the study we call chemistry.

ALCHEMY FACTS

The dawn of alchemy in Europe dates back to around 3500 BC, when people attempted to fire metals and combine them to make new ones. There are also stories of alchemists in India and China who tried to discover the links between fire, gold and eternal life.

CHEMISTRY OR MAGIC?

The business of ancient alchemists was making ornaments and jewellery out of precious metals like gold. Later, they tried to transform base metals, such as lead, into more precious ones, like gold. Alchemists understood how fire could be used to transform metals, and how to produce colours. In trying to make copper look like gold, they invented brass. In trying to make blue turquoise, they made a blue glaze that was the origin of glass. Over time, alchemy became known as a black art because the science behind it was not understood and people thought the transformations were the result of magic and witchcraft.

THE AIM OF ALCHEMY

The art of alchemy was practised throughout Europe, Egypt and Asia. Because the transformation of metals seems magical, alchemists also believed they could make a medicine, or elixir, which would allow the drinker to live forever. In Europe, alchemists tried to create a philosophers' stone, or a 'stone of the wise'. They believed that such a stone would transform ordinary matter into gold and bring immortal life to the owner.

The word alchemy comes from the Arabic word 'al-kīmiyā' meaning 'philosopher's stone'.

Legend has it that Chinese alchemists were in search of a potion that would bring eternal life, when they discovered black, fiery gunpowder.

The work of alchemists was often written in codes, cyphers and symbols, which partly explains why modern chemistry uses symbols to this day.

Of all four elements (earth, air, fire and water) the one with the greatest power over our planet is water. Water is like blood pumping through Earth's veins and without it there would be no life. Water is made of hydrogen and oxygen. Separately these elements are explosive but together, as water, they are harmless. But do not underestimate the power of water: it shapes the landscape, creates our weather systems, and was one of the reasons why modern human civilisations developed. Water flows over the planet's surface and deep underground, and it is present high in the air. It exists in three forms, as a solid, liquid or gas.

THE ORIGINS OF WATER

Where does all the water on Earth come from? After decades of searching for an answer, scientists now believe there's a vast reservoir of water, deep down inside the planet. There's enough water here to fill the Earth's oceans at least three times over! The reservoir is mostly trapped within rocks, hundreds of miles under the surface, but earthquakes and volcanoes from millions of years ago drove the water to the surface, which is how it appeared on Earth's surface.

DEEP DOWN

This deep reservoir of water isn't free-flowing. It is locked up 660 km (400 mi) below the planet's surface, in a mineral called ringwoodite which acts like a sponge. Water is made of two hydrogen atoms and one oxygen atom, which is why it's also called H_2O. Ringwoodite naturally attracts hydrogen atoms towards it and so it traps water molecules within it.

Ringwoodite has been found in a diamond, meaning these gems found deep underground could contain water!

The mineral ringwoodite appears in a few places within a larger rock or gem stone.

RINGWOODITE WEIGHT

Scientists found the first sample of the mineral ringwoodite within a diamond from Brazil. A study of the glistening gem showed that 1.5% of its weight was water. Although it sounds small, if all the millions of rocks and gems underground contained ringwoodite (and therefore water), it would prove that there are huge volumes of water beneath the surface of our planet!

COMETS

There was a time when we thought our planet's water was brought here by comets while the Earth was forming. But this new discovery of water deep beneath the surface suggests that Earth has always had water. Another reason why the comet theory is probably not true is because we now know that water comes in two types: normal and heavy (heavy water has more material inside its hydrogen atoms). Earth has mostly normal water, but the water found on comets is heavy, so it couldn't have made up the Earth's oceans.

Magma and gems containing ringwoodite are forced to the surface of the planet by geological activity such as volcanoes and earthquakes.

Subduction zone

THE TRANSITION ZONE

Understanding that water is held below Earth's surface in ringwoodite, means that there may be a major water source beneath the Earth's upper mantle, in an area known as the transition zone. Scientists studying a huge underground region lying underneath most of the United States believe that they may have found the evidence that explains how the vast oceans on the surface of Earth came to be.

Earth's upper mantle is made of plates which move around.

The Earth's lower mantle is made of solid rock. Temperatures here would normally cause rock to melt, but intense pressure pushing down from above has created a thick, gloopy magma.

RIVERS AND OCEANS

There's a huge amount of water on our planet, covering around 71% of Earth's surface. It flows in rivers, lakes, oceans, seas, swamps, ice caps, the atmosphere and through the ground. Most of this water, 96.5% of it, is in the salty oceans. The oceans are hugely important to life on Earth as they produce oxygen for us to breathe and they influence the weather systems. Although we give the oceans different names, they are actually all connected and water flows freely between them. All river water eventually ends up in the oceans as well.

THE SALTY OCEANS

There are very few people who are not dependent on the oceans in some way, even if they have never seen one. We eat fish from the ocean, lie on its beaches, swim in the waves, transport our goods in ships across them, and mine their floors for oil. There are definitely four oceans – the Arctic, Atlantic, Indian and Pacific – and most scientists agree there is a fifth ocean too. It's where the Atlantic, Indian and Pacific Oceans merge into the icy waters around Antarctica. There is no global agreement on the name of this fifth ocean, or where its boundaries lie, so it has a few names, including: the Antarctic, Austral or Southern Ocean.

Arctic

Atlantic

Pacific

Indian

Antarctic

The Yangtze River in China is home to the world's most powerful water-power plant. At its maximum capacity, the river can produce enough power to supply almost 10% of all Chinese households with electricity.

The Nile in Africa is thought to be the longest river in the world, but some experts suggest the Amazon River is longer, if you include the Pará **estuary** and connecting canal.

The Amazon River is the largest river in the world, based on volume of water. About one-fifth of all the fresh water flowing into the oceans in the world is from the Amazon.

FRESH WATER

If oceans make up 96.5% of the planet's surface water, the other 3.5% is freshwater. This is the water found in rivers and lakes, and the frozen water locked in **glaciers** and polar ice caps. Rivers have their source in lakes, springs, wetlands and glaciers. The fresh water flows through into tributaries, which are streams or rivers that flow into a larger main river. The main river then flows towards the coast, where its waters are emptied into the sea.

THE OXYGEN MADE BY OCEANS COMES FROM TINY ORGANISMS KNOWN AS PLANKTON. THEY MAKE OVER HALF THE OXYGEN THAT WE BREATHE!

In 2007 a Slovenian marathon swimmer, Martin Strel, became the first man to swim the entire length of the Amazon River. It took him 67 days, swimming 10 hours a day, with a team of 20 people protecting him from the creatures lurking under the water!

When talking about a river, 'upstream' means in the direction of the river's source. 'Downstream' means the direction the water is flowing, out to the end of the river.

Small rivers may also be called creeks, streams and brooks.

THE WATER CYCLE

Think about the water you have drunk today. How old do you think it is? Older than you? It may have fallen from the sky as rain about a week ago, but the water in your cup is basically as old as the Earth itself! The water on our planet today is the same water that was drawn from wells at the time of medieval kings and queens, or used by the ancient Egyptians, or even drunk by dinosaurs, millions of years ago. This is because all water is recycled over and over again in the water cycle.

WATER'S JOURNEY

A process called the water cycle has been moving water around the planet for more than four billion years. Water that is not locked up as ice is always on a journey – from land to sky and back again. The water cycle is made possible by water's ability to change easily from a liquid to a gas and back again.

Condensation

Evaporation from oceans, lakes and rivers

Transpiration from plants

EVAPORATION

Evaporation happens when liquid water turns into a gas. The Sun's energy heats up water in rivers, lakes or the ocean, and changes liquid water into water vapour (a gas). Plants and trees also lose water to the atmosphere through their leaves, in a process called transpiration. During evaporation and transpiration, warm water vapour rises into the sky.

CONDENSATION

Way up in the sky, water vapour cools down and turns back into liquid water droplets in a process called condensation. The droplets gather to form clouds. That's what clouds are – floating water! The atmosphere only stores about 1/1000th of the world's fresh water at any one time, but it can move water vapour around very quickly. There are even rivers in the sky! Low-lying clouds that carry a lot of water get blown along by strong winds to form these 'atmospheric rivers'.

PRECIPITATION

When enough water has condensed into water droplets, the droplets become too big and heavy for the clouds to hold them. We all know what happens next – the 'heavens open' and water falls back to Earth as rain, snow, sleet or hail. This is called precipitation. Precipitation that falls on land soaks into the earth and becomes ground water, which plants and animals drink. Or it runs over the soil and flows back into larger water bodies such as lakes, and the water cycle starts all over again.

Precipitation

THERE ARE THREE MAIN STAGES OF THE WATER CYCLE: EVAPORATION, CONDENSATION AND PRECIPITATION.

Water runs off the surface, into larger bodies of water.

ORIGINS OF LIFE

As we've learnt, water covers 71% of our planet, and every living thing needs water to exist. So it's no surprise that scientists believe all life on Earth started in water. They think that the first minuscule organisms probably appeared in the ocean around 3.8 billion years ago. These tiny organisms evolved gradually and eventually moved onto land about 450 million years ago.

1. Cold water seeps down through the rock at the bottom of the ocean.

Crust

2. When cold water meets hot rock in the crust, it causes cracks in the rock to deepen.

WHY WATER?

The word 'matrix' means an environment in which something can develop and thrive. Water is a perfect matrix for life. It is a calm and neutral substance, and it stays liquid over a wide range of temperatures. But water can also bond with other chemicals, and when certain chemicals are placed in water, they can react together. Water enables the kind of delicate chemistry that made the origins of life possible!

BLACK SMOKERS

Deep cracks in the ocean floor where there is volcanic activity, are called vents, or 'black smokers'. They look like chimneys, belching out black clouds of super-heated water, full of toxic chemicals. A black smoker is not a place where you would expect life to exist as there is no sunlight to allow plants to convert energy into carbon for creatures to eat. However, tiny bacteria live on these black smokers, getting their energy from chemicals in the water. Worms, mussels and clams feed on the bacteria, which allows larger fish to feed on them for their energy! Scientists believe this explains how the first living organisms came to exist on the planet.

4. Nutrient-rich hot water is forced through vents back into the ocean.

3. Water soaks through the cracked rocks, picking up nutrients from rocks below, which are heated up by magma in the upper mantle.

Upper mantle

DEEP DOWN

All this underwater activity is happening at a depth of 2,000 to 3,000 m (6,500 to 9,800 ft). Around the vents, the water may only be 2°C (36°F), but the heated water erupting out of the vents can be 60°C to 400°C (140-750°F)!

WATER AND LIFE

You, me and the other 7 billion human beings on this planet need water to survive. We need freshwater, the 3.5% of the planet's water that is free from salt. Humans can survive for three weeks without food, but only three days without water. It's little wonder when you think that more than 60% of our body is made up of water, and up to 78% of a newborn baby's body is water! But water is vital to more than just humans – it's the key to survival for every living thing on our planet.

TREE ROOTS CAN GROW 120 M (400 FT) DEEP LOOKING FOR WATER

TAKE ME TO THE WATER

Plants grow great distances in search of water. The deepest recorded tree roots reached 120 m (400 ft) below the Earth's surface. The roots belonged to a wild fig tree, which had grown deep into the Echo Caves in South Africa in search of a water source. It is thought that plants can even 'hear' water. A plant root will grow towards the sound of running water. This has inspired the design of space robots that can hunt for water and seek out life!

WATER, WATER, EVERYWHERE

A MATURE OAK TREE NEEDS UP TO 230 LITRES (60 GALLONS) OF WATER A DAY (THAT'S ABOUT THREE BATHTUBS FULL).

A CAMEL CAN DRINK 1.5 BATHTUBS OF WATER IN 13 MINUTES!

EVERY CELL NEEDS WATER

All animals need water, from farm animals, to wild animals and your family pet. They face different challenges when it comes to finding and using water, but just like us, they have devised ingenious ways of doing it. Camels can last up to 10 months without a drink, as long as they eat enough green vegetation and lick the dew from plants. And a thirsty camel can drink as much as 135 l (35 gal.) in about 13 minutes! This would kill most other animals, but camels have water storage sacks in their stomachs (not in their humps – they store fat in those!).

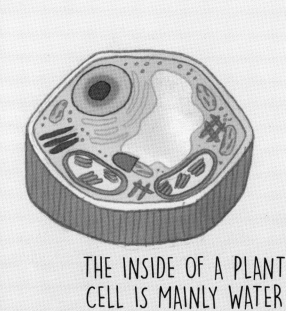

THE INSIDE OF A PLANT CELL IS MAINLY WATER

ADULTS ARE 60% WATER

BABIES ARE 78% WATER

A BANANA TREE IS 90% WATER

MADE OF WATER

All the wonderful life forms on Earth depend on access to water and cannot exist without it. Most plants are 80–90% water. Water is essential for seeds to sprout, and plants to grow. Water allows plants to absorb nutrients from the soil, and move nutrients between cells. Water also creates the pressure in plant cells which enables them to stand upright!

ICE AGES

Today, 30% of our planet's fresh water is locked up as ice, and most of this is contained in huge areas of ice at the poles. However, 12,000 years ago much of the Northern Hemisphere was covered in a single, vast ice sheet which had been there for thousands of years. A period of history such as this is called an ice age, and there have been many of them in our planet's history. When the temperature dropped and more of the planet's fresh water froze, the world was transformed. Our early ancestors had to learn how to adapt to the cold, to survive.

ICE IS A WATER BANK

During an ice age, there are enormous expanses of ice around the globe. When water has turned to ice, it is no longer liquid and can't easily evaporate. The water cycle we learnt about on pages 194-195 is affected and there is less precipitation to create ground water for plants and animals to drink.

COPING WITH ICE

During the last ice age, thick glaciers covered much of Europe, North America and Asia. Running water was scarce and these areas became too harsh for humans to survive. Even outside the ice-covered regions, many areas became drier as seas retreated. Fresh water was so scarce that survival became a real challenge. Other areas became wetter as creeping glaciers supplied meltwater. All of this triggered the movement of our ancestors around the world as they searched for better areas in which to live. You can read more about human migration on pages 56–65.

DURING THE ICE AGE, OUR ANCESTORS WENT IN SEARCH OF WATER. THESE WERE AMONG THE FIRST MIGRATIONS OF HUMANS AROUND THE WORLD.

THE SAHARA DESERT

The Sahara Desert is one of the driest places on Earth, but thousands of years ago this area of North Africa was a network of river valleys that criss-crossed the land. Prehistoric rock art in the Sahara shows giraffes and a host of other animals drinking water. But then, perhaps as a result of the Ice Age, the rivers dried up. There was less rainfall, rivers shrank and lakes dried out. The Saharans living in the area had no choice but to leave – they turned their back on their Saharan home and found water in new lands.

201

WATER AND FARMING

When the last ice age ended 12,000 years ago and more fresh water became unlocked from the melting ice, humans began to settle in one place rather than move around. The availability of more water led to the beginning of human civilisation as people started farming the land where they settled. Instead of going out to hunt, people used water around them to farm crops like wheat and barley, and began to feed and water certain animals. Villages sprang up as a result of this.

THE FIRST FARMERS

Farming started in the Fertile Crescent area in what is now called the Middle East. The area was blessed with easy access to water and edible crops that grew there naturally.

COLLECT THE WATER

The farming revolution meant humans didn't need to follow the seasonal rains, as hunter-gatherers had done. But they did need to collect water, for watering crops and looking after their animals.

ANIMAL LOTTERY

There are nearly two million species of animals on Earth, but only 14 mammals have ever been successfully farmed. They include goats, sheep, pigs, cows, horses, donkeys, Bactrian camels, Arabian camels, water buffalo, llamas, reindeer, yaks, mithuns and Bali cattle. Of these 14, the big four livestock animals – cows, pigs, sheep and goats – were all native to the Fertile Crescent! So the area that was home to the best crops in the world was also home to the animals most suited to farming. Little wonder that this was where people first lived in towns and cities, and human civilisation started.

THE SPREAD OF CIVILISATION

Any two points on the globe that share the same latitude (see page 220 for details about this) often have a similar climate and vegetation. San Francisco in the USA and Sicily in Italy are a good example. After human civilisation began in the Fertile Crescent it was only a matter of time before it started to spread. There was an explosion of farming along the same latitude as people moved east towards India, and west towards north Africa and Europe, building villages beside water sources.

RIVER CULTURE

As time passed and farming became an established way of life, people began to understand the importance of rivers. They built villages beside rivers, and grew seeds in wet mud along the riverbanks. As villages grew larger, farmers needed water to flow across a wider area of land so they could grow more crops and feed more people. They dug ditches which allowed water from flooding rivers to flow in new directions.

CITY LIFE

Villages that were built by rivers often became successful. The people who lived there became so good at farming that they grew more food than they needed to survive. In a small village, most people need to work on the land to grow food. But a large village can produce a lot of food and so not everyone needs to spend their time farming. In early large villages, people developed skills as craftsmen or traders. This is how town and eventually city life came to be organised, with people doing a variety of jobs.

INDUS VALLEY CIVILISATION

One of the first human civilisations was the Indus Valley civilisation, by the Indus river, around 5,000 years ago. This ancient society lay between present-day Pakistan and north-west India. At its peak, the Indus civilisation may have had a population of more than five million people, which means their cities must have been well planned. At the sites of the ancient cities of Mohenjo-Daro and Harappa there's lots of evidence of advanced plumbing and water culture! Many houses had wells and bathrooms, a water-supply system, drinking wells and elaborate drainage systems. One of the most impressive structures in Mohenjo-Daro was the Great Bath, which was the size of a swimming pool.

PADDY FIELDS

Our farming ancestors learnt how to use controlled flooding to their advantage. When the rains came, farmers would make no attempt to stop rivers from flooding their fields. The water carried nutrient-rich mud, or silt, and deposited it in a deep layer at the bottom of the field's basin. Rice grows perfectly in these conditions and it is believed this kind of wet-field farming originated in China.

ALMOST ALL EARLY VILLAGES, TOWNS AND CITIES GREW NEXT TO RIVERS OR BY THE SEA. IT'S THE SAME TODAY — CITIES SUCH AS LONDON, MELBOURNE AND NEW YORK SPRANG UP ALONG RIVERS.

THE NILE

Rivers run over a very small part of the planet's surface. But these rivers were magnets for early farmers as they provided a steady supply of freshwater. In many instances rivers helped to shape the civilisations that grew up along them. This power of rivers to shape history is best understood by looking at the civilisation that sprang up along the banks of the River Nile: ancient Egypt.

THE NILOMETER

Ancient Egypt wasn't all about pyramids and pharaohs. If there's one thing that made their civilisation tick it was a water device known as the Nilometer! The Nilometer measured the changing level of the Nile. Each year, when the River Nile flooded, the maximum height the water reached meant the Egyptians could predict how well their crops would grow. More grain meant more money for the farmers.

SILT IS LIKE A RICH SOUP OF MINERALS. IT IS MADE UP OF TINY FLECKS OF ROCK THAT RIVERS LIKE THE NILE PICK UP ON THEIR LONG JOURNEY AS THEY FLOW TOWARDS THE SEA.

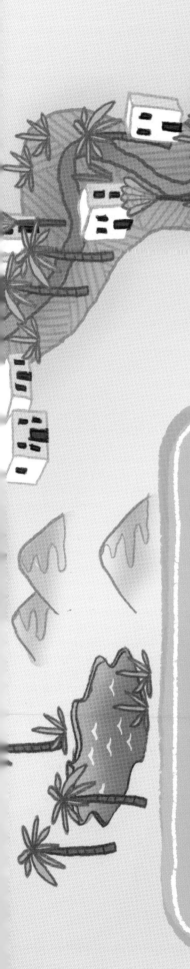

SHARING THE NILE

The Nile is believed by some to be the world's longest river. It runs through eleven countries: Tanzania, Burundi, Rwanda, Kenya, Uganda, Democratic Republic of the Congo, South Sudan, Ethiopia, Eritrea, Sudan and Egypt.

THE NILE'S FERTILE SECRET

Using the Nilometer to predict the growth of crops worked because the Nile carried a secret ingredient in its water – silt. All rivers carry silt, but the Nile is jam-packed with it. That's because this great river starts its journey in northeast Africa, where the volcanic rocks break down and create nutrient-rich silt. Almost 150 million tonnes of silt flows in the Nile waters each year. The annual Nile flooding of Egypt's fields meant the crops were covered with this nutrient-rich silt. The more silt that flowed, the more food grew!

SO SOCIETY FLOWS

Now we know: much of the wealth and power of ancient Egypt is because of the rich silt in the Nile. The silt was deposited on the land every year by the floodwaters and this helped produce an abundance of food. The Nile also influenced the structure of Egypt's society. Watering of the crops in ancient Egypt had to be organised on a large scale and many different people were needed to do different jobs. Managers decided where to dig the water channels. Workers did the digging. Then farmers bought and planted seeds in the fertile land, while others harvested and sold the crops.

THE HANGING GARDENS OF BABYLON

The Hanging Gardens of Babylon were one of the greatest man-made structures ever built. The gardens were one of the Seven Wonders of the Ancient World and the only 'wonder' that used water. Thought to have been built by the ancient Mesopotamian civilisation around 600 BC in present-day Iraq, the lush gardens were built high above the ground on multilayered mud-brick terraces. The gardens were said to be the most beautiful of sights, but sadly they no longer exist today and so we have to rely on stories about them.

The gardens probably needed 37,270 L (9,850 gal.) of water each day to keep the plants watered. That's the same as 466 bathtubs full!

Babylonia was ruled by King Nebuchadnezzar II and it is said he built the gardens for his wife.

The gardens were thought to be 23 m (75 ft) high.

THE WATER PROBLEM

The ancient Mesopotamians were experts with water. For many centuries they built canals and waterworks and their cities grew up around these. But building the Hanging Gardens must have been a huge design challenge even for these water experts. The Gardens needed thousands of litres of water every day, but Babylonia was a hot, dry place where it rarely rained. Although the Euphrates River was near by, engineers had to work out how to lift the river water into the air to reach the plants at the top. So if the Gardens really did exist, how on earth did people water them? This is the unanswered watery mystery of the Hanging Gardens!

The plants didn't actually 'hang', they grew on different levels, but the foliage spilled over the edge of each terrace.

An ingenious **irrigation** system carried water around the gardens, keeping the plants well watered every day.

SCREW PUMP

One possible solution to the water problem was the screw pump. When a screw pump is turned, water is caught between the blades of the screw and carried upwards. When the water reaches the top, it falls out into a pool at the higher level. As far as we know, the ancient Greek engineer, Archimedes, invented the screw pump around 250 BC which was more than 300 years after the Gardens were created! Although it's possible the Mesopotamians invented an early version.

WATER MEGACITY

The city of Angkor is a monument to the Khmer civilisation's mastery of monsoon rains. Over 1,000 years ago, a group of people called the Khmer settled by the Tonlé Sap Lake in present-day Cambodia. The Khmer knew that each year when the monsoon arrived the rainwaters flooded the land and flowed into the lake, which swelled enormously. When the monsoon ended, the water drained away and evaporated in the heat. The fish vanished leaving people hungry. To stop this pattern of flooding during one half of the year, and drought and hunger during the next, the Khmer built a huge network of canals around their capital city of Angkor, to spread the flood waters over the land and use it for farming. Angkor can still be seen today.

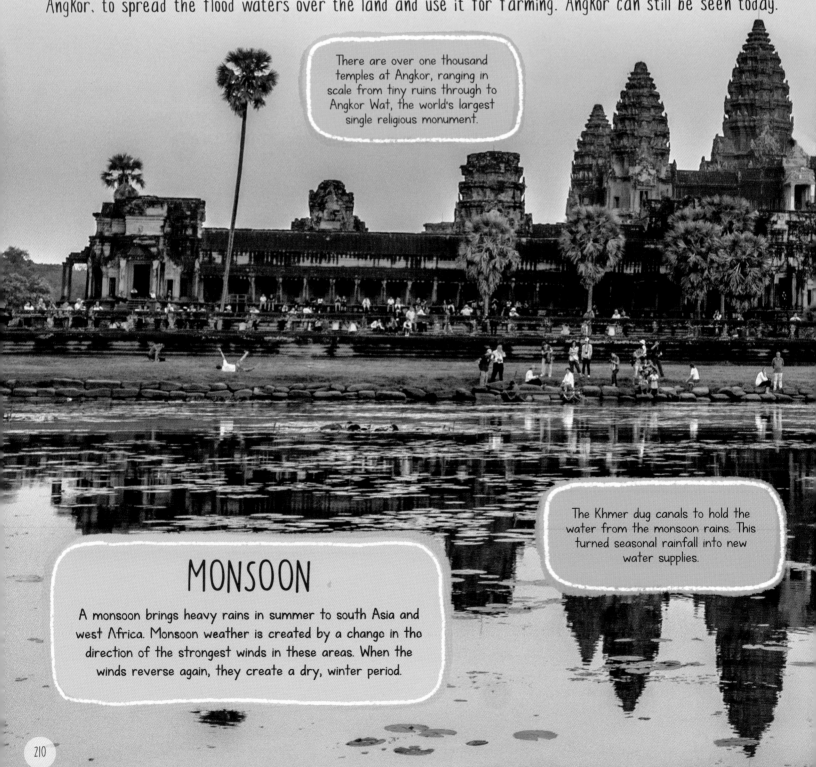

There are over one thousand temples at Angkor, ranging in scale from tiny ruins through to Angkor Wat, the world's largest single religious monument.

The Khmer dug canals to hold the water from the monsoon rains. This turned seasonal rainfall into new water supplies.

MONSOON

A monsoon brings heavy rains in summer to south Asia and west Africa. Monsoon weather is created by a change in the direction of the strongest winds in these areas. When the winds reverse again, they create a dry, winter period.

CITY WATERWAYS

The Khmer redirected the flow of a river by 80 km (50 mi) and built canals over an area of 1,000 km (400 sq mi). Thanks to their clever use of water, the Khmer built the largest pre-industrial city in the world, with a population of over one million people.

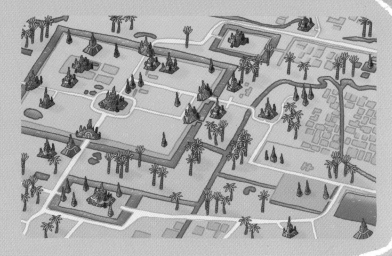

RICH WITH FISH

When the Tonlé Sap Lake floods with the monsoon rains it trebles in size and becomes the largest freshwater lake in Southeast Asia. And where there's water, there's fish. So much fish that it becomes the richest source of freshwater fish in the world!

The Khmer kingdom of Angkor was eventually a victim of its own success – the population grew so much that the water supply could no longer sustain them all!

THE KHMER EMPIRE RULED BETWEEN 802 AND 1431. AT ITS PEAK, THE EMPIRE COVERED MUCH OF SOUTHEAST ASIA INCLUDING CAMBODIA, THAILAND, LAOS AND SOUTHERN VIETNAM.

CANALS

A canal is a man-made waterway rather than a natural one such as a river. Ancient civilisations like the Egyptians, Mesopotamians and Indians all dug small canals into the banks of great rivers to help water their crops. Over the centuries, people have learnt to build all sorts of waterways to help them transport goods and people.

CHINA'S GRAND CANAL

The Chinese built the world's longest man-made waterway. The Grand Canal is 1,800 km (1,200 mi) long, and was dug completely by hand! It starts at Beijing and ends at Hangzhou, linking the Yellow and Yangtze rivers. The oldest parts were built in the 5th century BC and other sections were added almost a thousand years later. The Grand Canal is one of the planet's most awesome engineering projects and it is still used today.

FLOWING UPHILL

Water doesn't flow uphill so when a canal meets a hill or the level of the land rises, engineers need to find a way to move the water and anything on it, up! The solution is called a lock. A lock has two gates, and the water level on either side of the gates is different. To transport a boat uphill, you move it into the chamber at the lower level and close the first gate behind it. By opening a valve in the second gate, the water at the higher level flows into the chamber, lifting the boat up. Then, when you fully open the second gate, the boat floats onwards at the higher level.

INDUSTRIAL REVOLUTION

The Industrial Revolution in Britain happened between 1760 and 1840. Factories were built to produce goods on a bigger scale than ever before and these goods needed to be transported around the country. However, horses could only pull carts of a certain weight, and many roads were little more than mud tracks. A better transport system was needed to move goods around the country quickly. Canals were the answer! Because boats float, they could be loaded up with much more weight than a cart. A huge canal network was built all around the country.

YANG'S DREAM

The Grand Canal in China was commissioned by Emperor Yang. The main rivers in China ran west to east, but Yang wanted a canal to carry grain from the rich farming areas in the south to feed the capital cities and huge armies in the north. People thought he was mad, but with one million workers and thousands of soldiers he achieved his dream!

A. Boat sails in at the lower level

B. Gate 1 closes and gate 2 opens to fill the chamber with water

C. Boat rises up

D. Boat sails out at the higher level

Gate 1

Gate 2

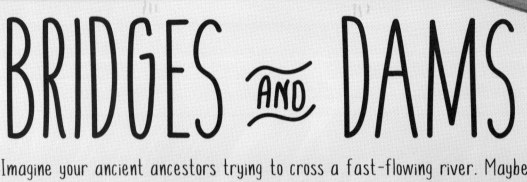

BRIDGES AND DAMS

Imagine your ancient ancestors trying to cross a fast-flowing river. Maybe they wanted to reach more fertile land on the other side. Or perhaps they needed to link up with another village. If the water was too dangerous to cross by boat, then a bridge would be the best way get across. Our ancient ancestors must have seen natural bridges made by fallen trees and realised they could easily build their own bridges.

WOODEN BRIDGES

Bridges were used in ancient times when the first civilisations rose up in places such as Mesopotamia and the Indus Valley. At first, they were very simple structures used to span small streams and rivers. They were built from wood, stone and dirt. They weren't very strong, as rain often dissolved the dirt fillings holding the bridge together.

CONCRETE BRIDGES

The ancient Romans caused a revolution in bridge building. Their engineers found that volcanic rocks could be mixed with sand, water and a natural paste called cement to create a mixture which, when it hardened, formed a strong, solid material called concrete. The discovery of concrete meant the Romans could build longer and stronger bridges, spanning larger rivers. The Romans also built amazing aqueducts – bridges which carried water.

LONG BRIDGES

Over the centuries, people gradually built bigger and better bridges. The longest bridge in the world is the Danyang-Kunshan Grand Bridge in China. It's about 165 km (102 mi) long, runs roughly parallel to the Yangtze River and threads through five cities.

OPENING BRIDGES

Tower Bridge crosses the River Thames in central London. It's not very high and sometimes tall ships need to pass under it to continue their journey upstream. Engineers devised a way to let boats pass underneath – the bridge splits in half and rises up in the middle!

DAMS

A dam is a barrier that stops water from flowing fully downstream. Water builds up behind the dam wall creating a large lake or resevoir. When the high pressure water behind the barrier is allowed to flow out, it can drive a turbine and create electricity (see page 235 for more information on how this works). The Hoover Dam in America is over 200 m (700 ft) high and it generates electricity for the local states.

EXPLORING THE SEAS

We know that some of our ancient ancestors had the desire to explore the world around them. This is why people migrated by land, discovering and populating new continents – see page 56 onwards for detail about human migration. Exploring the world by sea was a far more challenging task. For one thing, people needed to build seaworthy boats and ships. Unlike journeys over land, once our ancestors set off on water they couldn't necessarily stop when they felt like it. And to survive at sea they had to take everything with them!

THE SEVEN SEAS

You've probably heard the phrase 'sailing the seven seas'. It came into use when the ancient Greeks set out to explore the world by sea. For them, the seven seas were situated around the Mediterranean Sea and were the waters of the Aegean, Adriatic, Mediterranean, Black, Red and Caspian seas. In different cultures at different times, the 'seven seas' has been used to mean waters along trade routes, waters in a certain region, or exotic, faraway waters. Today, the seven seas generally refers to the Arctic, North Atlantic, South Atlantic, North Pacific, South Pacific, Indian and Southern Oceans.

WET ROUTES

Exploring the seas allowed people to trade their goods. Take the Indian Ocean as an example. This ocean was the watery equivalent of the Silk Road, the ancient network of trade routes that went over land linking the East and West. The Indian Ocean trade routes connected the east coast of Africa with empires in the Middle East, India, China and Southeast Asia via key port cities. The Indian Ocean trade was bigger, richer and included more countries than the Silk Road. Trade between countries boomed in the 14th and 15th centuries.

The Silk Road

THE MONSOON MARKETPLACE

The monsoon winds that blow over the Indian Ocean are very predictable. A sea captain could rely on the monsoon winds to fill his sails from Africa to India between April and September, and then bring the ship back to Africa if he sailed between November and February. See page 210 for more information on the monsoon.

Wet trade routes

ZHENG HE AND THE CITY ON WATER

Zheng He was a Chinese admiral in the 15th century. Between 1405 and 1433 he led voyages over the Indian Ocean. Zheng He's fleet of ships was like a city on water. There were more than 300 ships with a crew of over 27,000 sailors – more than half of London's population at the time. Some of these ships were enormous! The flagships (known as the treasure ships) were over 120 m (400 ft) long and had seven or more masts.

THE AGE OF EXPLORATION

The modern age of exploration, when people from different parts of the globe began to link up, really began with the sea voyages of the 15th century. In Europe, it was the Portuguese who first set off to sea, around the year 1415. They'd heard of the trade routes in the Indian Ocean and wanted to make money by opening up a new trade route by sea. At first, they sailed close to the coastlines because they were wary of open water. They crept along the coast of West Africa, each voyage going a little further than the one before.

AROUND THE WORLD ON WATER

In the 15th century, when sailors set sail for China, they sailed around Africa and headed east. Today, because we know that the world is round, we know you can also sail to China by travelling west from Europe. But 500 years ago people thought the world was flat! So who was to say what might happen if you sailed west from Europe into the open ocean? You might sail on and on without end or you might just drop off the edge of the Earth! There were no written records about routes leading west and people were scared of what lay across the Atlantic Ocean.

THE FAMOUS PORTUGUESE EXPLORER, VASCO DA GAMA, EVENTUALLY ARRIVED IN INDIA IN 1497 BY CREEPING DOWN AND AROUND THE AFRICAN COAST.

COLUMBUS

The Italian explorer and navigator, Christopher Columbus, knew he could reach China by travelling due east over land from Europe. But he wondered if he could also reach it by sailing west from Europe? Or would he find new lands his people didn't know about? Instead of sailing around Africa, Columbus caused a stir by setting sail directly west across the Atlantic. He found land, but it wasn't China, it was America – which no one from Columbus' part of the world knew existed! Soon, word spread of a 'New World' – a different continent, across the Atlantic Ocean.

LEIF THE LUCKY

Columbus was adventurous, but he may also have heard old stories about a Viking ocean explorer, who discovered land that lay to the west. Leif Erikson was an Icelandic Viking, born in 970, and the man believed to be the first known European to discover North America. He sailed to the northern tip of Newfoundland, in modern-day Canada, and his stories about this land were passed down through generations of Vikings, and possibly to Columbus.

WHY HIM?

There were many adventurous sailors in the 15th and 16th centuries such as Zheng He and Vasco da Gama, so why does everyone only remember Columbus from this period? It may be because, after Columbus reached America, the Northern Hemisphere was finally mapped. Groups of people who'd never met due to being separated by the seas could now interact just as we all do today! But Columbus also brought back new kinds of food from the west, such as potatoes, cacao, tomatoes and maize.

LATITUDE AND LONGITUDE

After Columbus, the Atlantic Ocean was thrown open to exploration by Europeans. There was a huge expansion in trade and the chance to discover more of the Americas. This triggered huge competition between nations. All the major trade routes were across the seas, and the race to reach new land and be the first to trade was fierce. Whether you were first to arrive or not, depended on the speed of your ship and the accuracy of your measurements: it became very important to know exactly where on the planet and how far away from your destination you were. The race for longitude and latitude had begun!

SAIL THE OPEN SEA

Imagine being the European captain of a ship at sea – your mission is to get to the Americas before your European rivals. The problem is that water isn't like land – you can't use landmarks to find your way. Sailors charted their course at sea by calculating the position of the Sun and the stars. This helped them to work out how far down the globe they were (latitude). But they needed more than that to work out how far across the globe they were (longitude).

+90 degrees latitude

+60 degrees latitude

+30 degrees latitude

Northern Hemisphere

0 degrees latitude

Equator ↗

-30 degrees latitude

Southern Hemisphere

-60 degrees latitude

-90 degrees latitude

Angle = degree of latitude

FINDING LATITUDE

Finding your latitude at sea is relatively easy. When the Sun is at its highest point in the sky at noon, you measure the angle between the Sun and the horizon. At night, in the Northern Hemisphere, you can do the same by using the position of the North Star in the sky.

TIME EQUALS LONGITUDE

When it is noon on one side of the Earth, it is midnight on the other. To work out longitude, scholars drew lines between these two points which were equal to a time difference of one hour. A ship could then find out how far east or west it was from home, by comparing the local time on board with the time back home at that instant. The problem was, clocks in the 17th century only worked when on solid land, so how could people tell the time on a rolling ship? A new invention was required.

LONGITUDE

The consequences were very serious if a captain or navigator miscalculated their position at sea. A ship could easily run into rocks and sink, with loss of life to all on board, but also loss of the cargo. Enormous prizes, worth millions in today's money, were offered to anyone who could figure out a way to calculate longitude at sea. Sailors and scientists all over Europe did their best to solve the problem, and when they did, it was one of the most important scientifc discoveries in history.

AND THE WINNER IS...

Many people came up with solutions to the problem of longitude and keeping track of the time at sea, but the prize was won by an English carpenter named John Harrison. He invented a mechanical clock that kept track of time at sea!

-30 degrees longitude (noon – 2 hrs)

0 degrees longitude (noon)

+30 degrees longitude (noon + 2 hrs)

+60 degrees longitude (noon + 4 hrs)

+90 degrees longitude (noon + 6 hrs)

+120 degrees longitude (noon + 8 hrs)

A NEW WAY OF THINKING ABOUT NATURE BEGAN WITH THE AGE OF EXPLORATION. PEOPLE STARTED QUESTIONING EXISTING BELIEFS. FOR EXAMPLE, SAILORS DISCOVERED THAT THE WORLD WAS NOT FLAT, AS HAD BEEN BELIEVED BY SOME.

PIRATES!

The Golden Age of Piracy was from 1650 to 1730, when sea captains were always on the lookout for pirates. Pirates were criminals sailing the seas who had their eyes on other ships' treasure. The most famous pirates sailed the Caribbean Sea and along the coasts of South and Central America, but there were also pirates waiting to attack the shipping lanes in the Indian Ocean. Pirates would plan their raids on merchant ships carrying expensive goods in the hope that they could sell them on and get rich quick!

BLACK BART

One of the most successful pirates was Bartholomew 'Black Bart' Roberts, who was born in Wales and who captured over 470 ships in his career! He used two different flags during his time at sea.

RED OR BLACK?

Ships always flew flags as identification. The traditional pirate flag was the 'Jolly Roger', but many pirates had their own distinct flags. In the early 18th century, if you saw a pirate flag that was black, it meant the pirates would show mercy if you gave up your ship. But if you saw a red flag it meant a fight to the death!

This Jolly Roger flag design was the most commonly used pirate flag in the 1720s.

PIRATE SHIPS

Pirates generally used ships called sloops. A sloop had a shallow bottom which made it perfect for hiding out in shallow, secluded bays where bigger ships couldn't follow.

PIRATES AND PRIVATEERS

Pirates capturing other ships and stealing their cargo were criminals. But if you were employed by a European country to do the same job as a pirate, you were a law-abiding sailor known as a privateer! So, what was the difference?

PIRATE

Sailors who robbed ships on the high seas, keeping the treasure for themselves.

BUCCANEER

English and French pirates, based on the islands of Tortuga (now part of Haiti) and Jamaica, in the 17th century. They mainly attacked Spanish ships in the area.

PRIVATEER

Sailors who stole on behalf of the government of a country and who carried a 'letter of marque', which meant they were legally allowed to take enemy ships. Many privateers eventually became pirates and buccaneers.

A PIRATE'S LIFE

Pirates spent most of their lives at sea. They were excellent sailors and their navigational skills meant they often escaped capture. They were experts too in the use of maps and the compass, and often stole a ship's instruments as well as its treasure. Many pirates first went to sea as sailors in the navy, but life on board a naval ship was extremely tough and sometimes the crew revolted against the captain! Then the sailors claimed the ship as their own, creating new rules. Their lives as pirates had begun!

223

EXPLORING RIVERS

Between the 15th and 18th centuries, European adventurers were not only curious about the seas, but also the waterways that lay inland. They began to explore and map the rivers of the world. Rivers have influenced the way our ancestors survived, and thrived, and we're still exploring them today.

TOP TEN LARGEST RIVERS IN THE WORLD

1. RIVER NILE, AFRICA

British explorer John Hanning Speke documented the source of the River Nile on 3rd August 1858. He named it Lake Victoria, after Queen Victoria, even though local people had called it something else for thousands of years. The first people to travel the entire length of the Blue Nile and the White Nile only did so recently, in 2004.

2. AMAZON RIVER, SOUTH AMERICA

The Amazon is the longest river in South America. The first recorded navigation of the entire length of the river was in 1542 by the Spanish explorer, Don Francisco de Orellana. He named the river after himself, but this was changed to *Rio Amazonas*, after the mythical tribe of warrior women. There were millions of people living in the Amazonian region at the time.

4. MISSISSIPPI RIVER, USA

Native American people have lived along the Mississippi River and its tributaries for over 10,000 years. Most were hunter-gatherers, but some established farming communities. One of the largest of these communities had as many as 20,000 people living in it, almost 2,000 years ago.

3. YANGTZE RIVER, CHINA

Also known as Chang Jiang, this is the longest river in Asia. There is evidence of our ancient ancestors living in the area as far back as 2 million years ago.

5. YENISEI RIVER, RUSSIA

The Yenisei flows from a sacred mountain in central Mongolia, through grasslands and canyons in Siberia, and north to the Arctic Ocean.

6. YELLOW RIVER, CHINA

The name comes from the huge amounts of yellow sediment in the water. For thousands of years, the river has been known as the 'mother river' because its basin was the birthplace of the ancient Chinese civilisation. The area around the Yellow River was the most prosperous region in China as far back as 2100 BC.

7. OB RIVER, RUSSIA

This river of central Russia is one of the great rivers of Asia. The amazing thing about the Ob is that it freezes over completely for 5-6 months of the year. Then, people ski, snowshoe or drive dog teams on the frozen river.

8. PARANÁ RIVER, SOUTH AMERICA

The warm climate of the Paraná is home to an abundance of wildlife, including the sabretooth anchovy, and the jaguar which prowls the river banks. This is the second longest river in South America.

9. CONGO RIVER, AFRICA

This river and its tributaries run through seven African countries. In 1482, Portuguese explorer Diego Cao became the first European to find the source of the Congo River.

10. AMUR RIVER, EAST ASIA

In 1639, a group of explorers led by Ivan Moskvitin became the first modern Russians to reach the Pacific Ocean. Having built a winter camp on its shore they learnt from the locals about the large Amur River. In 1640 they sailed south, explored the southeastern shores of the Okhotsk Sea and reached the mouth of the Amur River.

HIDDEN RIVERS

Just as adventurers 500 years ago set off on dangerous journeys in search of new rivers, explorers are still doing the same today. The exploration of rivers continues all over the world as there is still much to be discovered. Many rivers can be seen easily, but others are hidden underground, like the Hamza in South America.

UNDERGROUND RIVERS

Hidden rivers are special because, although we cannot see them directly, they carry huge amounts of water around in river systems under the ground. Sometimes they flow through underground caves, and at other times they seep through the soil and porous rock. See pages 18-19 for more about rock types.

Precipitation falls as rain

Porous rock

Water seeps into the Hamza River through holes in the rocks underneath the Amazon River.

DISCOVERING THE HAMZA RIVER

The Amazon River basin in South America is maybe the largest river system in the world, covering more than 7 million km² (2.7 million sq mi). But until recently, we only knew half the story. In 2011, the discovery of the Hamza River was announced to the world. The Hamza is a huge and hidden underground river that flows along roughly the same path as the famous Amazon, but about 4 km (2.5 mi) below it, under layers of rock. We now know that the Amazon basin empties into both the Amazon River and the Hamza River, in one gigantic flow of water.

HOW DID THEY FIND IT?

The Hamza was discovered by a team of Brazilian scientists, headed by Professor Hamza. They used data from a series of 241 abandoned deep wells that were drilled in the Amazon region by an oil company in the 1970s and 80s and found water flowing horizontally rather than vertically below a certain depth. The Hamza is 6,000 km (4,000 mi) long and ranges from 200 to 400 km (120 to 250 mi) wide.

The Amazon River ranges from 1 to 100 km (0.6 to 62 mi) wide at different points.

THE RIVER DEBATE

Is the Hamza actually a river? Some scholars think not! That's because researchers involved with the Hamza discovery say that water is moving through the porous rock under the Amazon at only a few centimetres a year. So they believe this is not a river flow in the usual sense. Water in the Amazon River flows at a speed of 5 m (16 ft) per second, but in the Hamza it flows at a speed of less than 1 mm (0.04 in) per hour. What do you think? Does a river have to flow at a particular speed to be called a river?

EXPLORING ICE

The poles of our planet are covered in ice. The North Pole sits at the top of the world, at the centre of the Northern Hemisphere. The South Pole sits at the bottom and is the centre of the Southern Hemisphere. Even though they are at the opposite ends of the planet, they share many things in common - they both have almost 24 hours of daylight for six months of the year, and 2-3 months of constant darkness. However, the South Pole lies on a continent, known as Antarctica, whereas the North Pole lies on sea ice in an area called the Arctic.

THE ARCTIC

The Arctic area at the north of the planet is actually the ice-covered Arctic Ocean and the surrounding land. This includes all of Greenland and Spitsbergen, and the northern regions of Alaska, Canada, Norway and Russia.

THE ARCTIC OCEAN

Water flows into the Arctic Ocean from both the Pacific and Atlantic Oceans. It makes up about 1.3% of the 'world ocean'. Much of the Arctic is covered by sea ice, which varies in thickness and size depending on the seasons. The sea ice is moved about by wind and ocean currents, and icebergs often break off from the ice sheet, posing a hazard to ships. From October to June each year the surface of the Arctic Ocean completely freezes over. Ships used to get trapped if they didn't leave before the water froze, but now modern icebreaker ships carve routes through the ice.

NORTH POLE

THE ARCTIC

Russia

Alaska (USA)

Canada

ICE ON LAND AND SEA

In the east of Antarctica, the ice sheet covers a huge area of land which is the continent of Antarctica – it's bigger than Australia! In the west of Antarctica, the ice sheet covers the sea and it is frozen to more than 2.5 km (1.5 mi) below sea level.

THE WORLD OCEAN

After centuries of study and exploration, we now know that the oceans of the world are all connected, making a 'world ocean' that covers 71% of the Earth's surface.

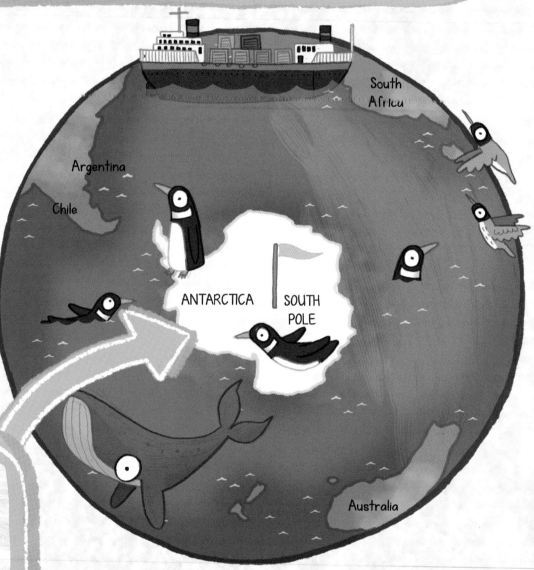

South Africa

Argentina

Chile

ANTARCTICA

SOUTH POLE

Australia

ANTARCTIC ICE SHEET

The Antarctic ice sheet covers 98% of Antarctica. The sheet is the largest single mass of ice on the planet! In fact, over 60% of all fresh water on Earth is held in the sheet. If it all melted tomorrow, it would cause a massive 58-m (190-ft) rise in sea level!

ICE AGES

Throughout Earth's history there have been ice ages – turn to pages 200-201 to read more about them. This is when the temperature of the planet plummets, the polar ice sheets expand, and much more of Earth's water is locked up in ice than it is today, meaning sea levels are lower. There have been at least five major ice ages in Earth's history. In fact, some scholars say we are still living in one which started 2.6 million years ago because we currently have ice sheets at the poles! Outside the ice ages, the planet is free from ice, even on the highest mountain-tops.

THE DEEP

The deep ocean remains one of the most mysterious places on Earth. We know less about these points on our planet than we do about the surface of Mars. Freezing cold, blacker than black, and with crushing pressures, the deepest part of the ocean is one of the most hostile places on the planet. What's it like down there, and what kind of creatures manage to survive there?

GOING DOWN

To get to the ocean's deepest point, we're going to have to plunge more than 10,000 m (32,800 ft) below the surface of the water.

3,000 m (9,850 ft)
We're going past the deepest point that sperm whales have ever been spotted.

3,800 m (12,500 ft)
Down we go, past the wreck of the RMS Titanic which sank tragically in 1912.

8,848 m (29,029 ft)
It's amazing to think about, but if you put all of Mount Everest on the bottom of the ocean, it would still be submerged with more than 1.6 km (1 mi) to go before you reached sea level!

THE MARIANA TRENCH

These are the long, narrow chasms at the very bottom of the world's oceans. Ocean trenches are found in every ocean on the planet, but the Mariana Trench in the western Pacific is the deepest of all. And the deepest point in the trench is Challenger Deep. The pressure of all that water here is over 1,000 times greater than at sea-level. That's strong enough to crush and dissolve most bones or shells, so any creatures that live in these murky waters are serious survivors.

10,995 m (36,073 ft)
The deepest point on Earth is known as Challenger Deep. The craft Deepsea Challenger travelled to the bottom in 2.5 hours in 2012.

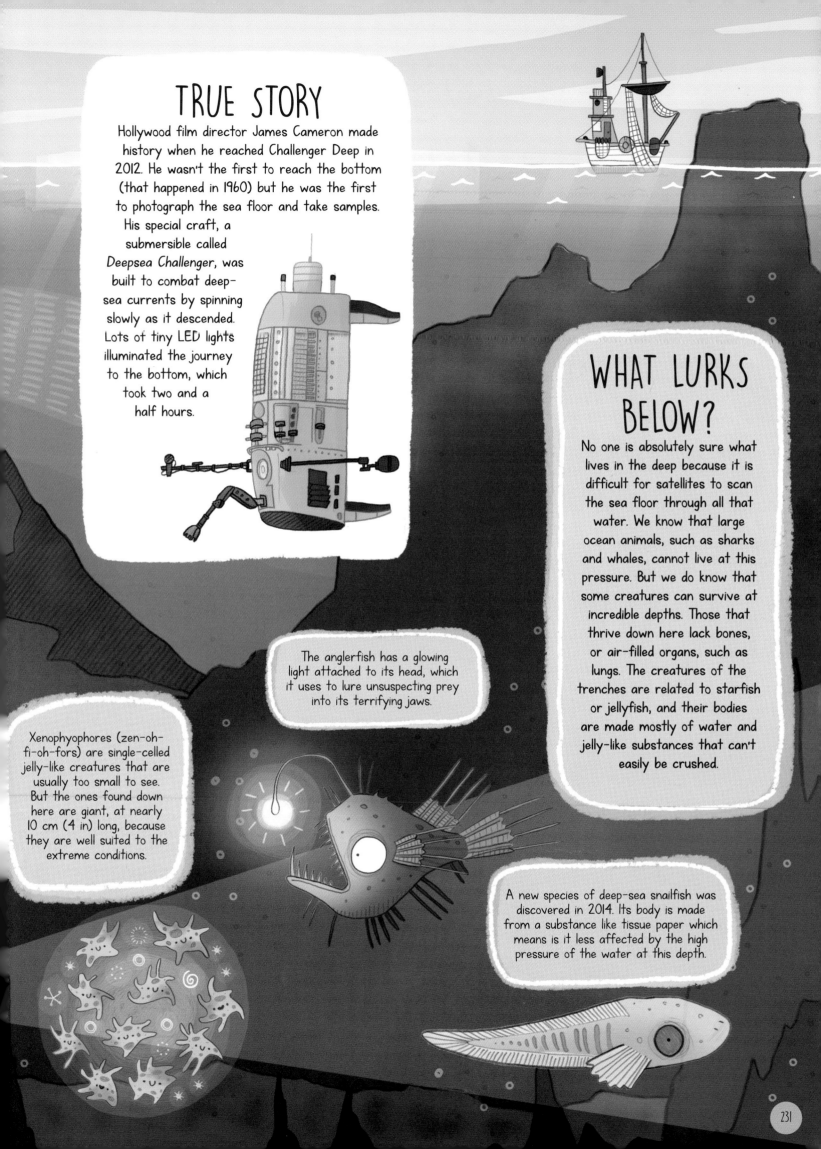

TRUE STORY

Hollywood film director James Cameron made history when he reached Challenger Deep in 2012. He wasn't the first to reach the bottom (that happened in 1960) but he was the first to photograph the sea floor and take samples. His special craft, a submersible called *Deepsea Challenger*, was built to combat deep-sea currents by spinning slowly as it descended. Lots of tiny LED lights illuminated the journey to the bottom, which took two and a half hours.

WHAT LURKS BELOW?

No one is absolutely sure what lives in the deep because it is difficult for satellites to scan the sea floor through all that water. We know that large ocean animals, such as sharks and whales, cannot live at this pressure. But we do know that some creatures can survive at incredible depths. Those that thrive down here lack bones, or air-filled organs, such as lungs. The creatures of the trenches are related to starfish or jellyfish, and their bodies are made mostly of water and jelly-like substances that can't easily be crushed.

The anglerfish has a glowing light attached to its head, which it uses to lure unsuspecting prey into its terrifying jaws.

Xenophyophores (zen-oh-fi-oh-fors) are single-celled jelly-like creatures that are usually too small to see. But the ones found down here are giant, at nearly 10 cm (4 in) long, because they are well suited to the extreme conditions.

A new species of deep-sea snailfish was discovered in 2014. Its body is made from a substance like tissue paper which means is it less affected by the high pressure of the water at this depth.

WATER AND CHANGE

Water is a life-giving liquid but it also has great power to change and shape the landscape. One of the subtle ways in which water uses its power is through weathering and erosion. Weathering is when rocks are broken and worn away over time. This forms part of the rock cycle, which you can read more about on pages 18-19. Erosion is when rocks and sediments are picked up and moved, and gradually worn down, by water, ice, wind or gravity.

PHYSICAL WEATHERING

Physical weathering is when water running over rocks, seeps in. When the temperature drops dramatically it causes the water to freeze. Frozen water takes up more space than liquid and forces cracks to appear in the rocks. The rock in this photo is called Split Apple Rock and it lies off the coast of New Zealand. Physical weathering also happens when rocks are baked by the Sun and are cracked by the heat.

CHEMICAL WEATHERING

Sometimes chemical reactions happen in water and cause changes in rocks. In warm, wet places for instance, water and oxygen sometimes work together to break down the minerals that make up rocks. And when water in clouds mixes with high levels of carbon dioxide in the air, the rain that falls becomes slightly acidic (see page 174). When it comes into contact with certain types of rock such as limestone or chalk, the rock starts to dissolve. This is how underground caves are created, as the rock is gradually dissolved over thousands of years.

SINKHOLES

When groundwater seeps underground and reaches water-soluble rock underneath, such as chalk or limestone, the water gradually erodes the rock and creates a sinkhole. Sometimes, the hole is covered by a layer of soil on the surface and when this layer can no longer support its own weight over the hole, it suddenly collapses. If a sinkhole appears suddenly in a town or city, it can cause enormous damage.

EROSION

Moving water also helps to break down rocks into smaller pieces, as fast-flowing water causes them to bash against each other over huge distances. The rocks erode as they are carried along and become rounder, which is why many pebbles in water are smooth to the touch! Rivers running in the mountains have lots of energy as they flow downhill towards the sea. As rocks travel down the river they erode the riverbeds and banks to create valleys that are shaped like the letter 'V'.

Fast-flowing water moves rocks along.

GLACIERS

During the last ice age, when the landscape was buried under sheets of ice, some parts of the Northern Hemisphere were almost 2 km (1.2 mi) deep in ice. Due to the forces of gravity, the heavy ice gradually began to slide downhill, carving away the land as it moved. When this happens it is called a glacier. Some glaciers were so huge that they carved out entire valleys from the rock.

A cirque is a bowl-shaped valley which sits at the head of a glacier.

A hanging valley is a U-shaped valley off to the side of a main glacial valley. They are created by smaller glaciers running off the sides of large ones.

A fjord is a narrow inlet of ocean, which sits between steep cliffs that have been carved by glaciers.

TIDES

Tides are the rising and falling movement of the sea. At different times of day, the water level against the shore might be higher or lower. The reason this happens is because seawater is influenced by the Sun's and Moon's gravity! High tides occur when the Moon's gravity pulls the water in the oceans nearest it towards it ever so slightly, causing the water to bulge out. The Earth itself is also pulled a little by the Moon, so the water furthest from the Moon is left behind and also bulges into a high tide. Low tides occur because the water on the top and bottom of Earth (when viewed in relation to the Moon, like in the main image on this page) is pulled away into the two bulging areas.

Low tide

High tide

High tide

Low tide

TIDAL POWER

Tidal power is incredibly powerful. Millions of litres of water move towards and then away from the shore over the space of a few hours. The currents created under the surface of the tides can also travel thousands of kilometres. People have wanted to tap the power in tides for many years and engineers are trying different technologies to harness this never-ending source of energy.

NEAP TIDES

When the Moon is a half moon in the sky, the Sun and Moon don't line up. They are at right angles, or 90 degrees, to each other, in relation to the Earth. That means their forces of gravity work against each other to make neap tides. Neap tides occur twice a month, and are lower than usual.

SPRING TIDES

The Sun also has an influence on our tides. When the Moon is new or full, the Sun, Earth and Moon line up and the gravity of the Sun and the Moon join forces to cause spring tides. This happens twice every month and the tides are higher than normal.

Spring tide

Neap tide

Neap tide

Spring tide

TIDAL TURBINES

Tidal currents run along the shore at depths of about 20 to 30 m (65 to 100 ft). Tidal turbines are a little like wind turbines, but their rotors are underwater. The rotors, each about 20 m (65 ft) wide, spin as tidal currents surge past, which turns a generator and makes electricity.

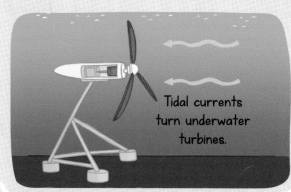

Tidal currents turn underwater turbines.

TIDAL BARRAGE

Another way to use the energy of all that moving water is to build a type of dam known as a barrage across a river or entrance to a bay. As water flows in and out at high and low tide, the flow across the turbines turns a generator, which makes electricity.

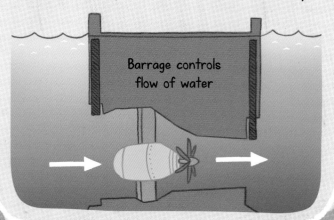

Barrage controls flow of water

TSUNAMI

Waves are created when energy passes through water. The energy is often created by wind or the tides, or when something makes the water move (like a ball hitting the surface, or an earthquake happening on the ocean floor). Children love to play in shallow ocean waves at the beach and surfers love to ride them, but some waves are deadly. They're known as tsunamis. A tsunami is a series of waves that send huge surges of water onto the land. These sheer walls of water, some up to 30 m (100 ft) high, come crashing down onshore, causing havoc and destruction on land.

READ THE WATER

Before a tsunami hits, there will often be clues that it is on the way. All waves have peaks and troughs, and with tsunamis it's the trough that arrives on land first. Tsunami troughs seem to suck coastal water out to sea, exposing the sea or harbour floor. This seawater retreat is a vital warning that danger is on its way.

3. As the water reaches the coast the waves get closer together and higher.

2. The height of waves at the place of origin are only small.

1. An earthquake hits, the seabed rises up and the water around it is moved, creating waves.

WHY AND WHERE?

Tsunamis are normally created by undersea earthquakes, which happen at tectonic plate boundaries (see pages 24-25). Underwater landslides and volcanic eruptions also cause them. In fact, 80% of tsunamis happen in the Pacific Ocean's 'Ring of Fire', an area where tectonic activity, such as earthquakes and volcanoes, is quite common. You don't get much warning with a tsunami. They can race across the ocean at speeds of up to 800 km/h (500 mph) - as fast as a jet plane!

HIGH AND MIGHTY

Out in the deep ocean, tsunami waves start out as only 50 cm (20 in) or so in height. But as they surge their way to the shoreline, the water gets shallower, causing the tsunami to slow down and grow in height. The tops of tsunamis move faster than their bases, and that causes them to rise steeply into terrifying towering peaks.

Wave peak

4. Water is sucked away from the coast before a wave up to 50 m (165 ft) high hits the shore.

Wave trough

MEGA-TSUNAMI

Some tsunamis are so huge they've been christened 'mega-tsunamis', although none have occurred in recent history. Some scientists think that if the Cumbre Vieja volcano in the Canary Islands erupts, it will release 500 cubic km (120 cubic mi) of rock straight into the sea. That would set off an enormous wave 1,000 m (3,280 ft) high. The wave would leave the Canary Islands and eventually hit Brazil, Britain and eastern USA. Even though the wave would lose height as it travelled, it could still be up to 50 m (165 ft) high when it reaches land and would cause huge destruction.

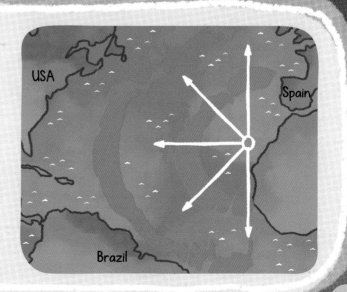

USA

Spain

Brazil

WATERFALLS

Waterfalls are a spectacular example of water's power. They happen when a river falls over a steep, rocky ledge and cascades into a plunge pool below. Some waterfalls form when the rock of a riverbed is eroded over time. The soft rock is gradually worn away by weathering (see pages 232-233), leaving behind a ledge of hard rock for the river to fall over. There are different kinds of waterfall, it all depends how the water falls!

THE SPEED OF THE FLOW OF WATER IN A RIVER INCREASES AS IT NEARS A WATERFALL. THAT MEANS IT HAS EXTRA POWER WHEN IT FALLS, FROM ALL THAT RAPID WATER RUNNING OVER THE EDGE

WATERFALLS AND EROSION

Flowing rivers carry sediment, which can be tiny particles of silt, hard stones or large boulders. Fast-moving sediment erodes riverbeds made of soft rock, such as limestone and sandstone. In time, the river cuts so deep into the soft rock, that only hard rock, such as granite, is left.

FAN WATERFALL

Here, the water fans out as it falls. Virgin Falls on Vancouver Island, Canada is a spectacular example.

BLOCK WATERFALL

A block waterfall falls in a wide stream. A good example of this is Niagara Falls, in Canada and the USA.

CASCADE WATERFALL

These waterfalls are ones in which the water falls over a series of steps. The Monkey Falls in India has shallow steps with such gently flowing water that children play here.

FROZEN WATERFALL

The clue is in the name! This is a waterfall that is frozen solid, for at least some of the year. The Fang in Colorado is a single column of ice that drops more than 30 m (100 ft).

CATARACT WATERFALL

A cataract means a powerful, often dangerous, type of fall. One of the wildest examples are the deafening cataracts of Iguazú Falls, which lie between Argentina and Brazil.

CHUTE WATERFALL

A chute waterfall is very narrow, and the water is forced over a ledge at high pressure. Three chute falls flow through the Yosemite National Park, in California, USA.

HYDROPOWER

All this falling water doesn't go to waste. Around the world, people are harnessing the flow of waterfall water in hydropower plants. The power plants convert the water's flow into electricity by running it through a turbine, which turns a generator. Worldwide, hydropower plants generate almost a quarter of the Earth's electricity, supplying power to more than 1 billion people.

THE RAINBOW

A rainbow is a beautiful sight. The spectacle of the rainbow is so stunning it has inspired many fairytales, songs and legends and evoked a sense of wonder in people the world over. But understanding how a rainbow works is really quite simple. It's a wonderful combination of water and light, which line up to create colours in the sky.

A RAINBOW'S SECRET

The two vital ingredients for a rainbow are raindrops and sunlight. The sunlight that we see appears white, but it is actually made up of seven different colour wavelengths that we can't normally see: red, orange, yellow, green, blue, indigo and violet. When sunlight passes through a raindrop at a certain angle, the different colours in the white sunlight separate into the seven colours. A rainbow forms when the seven colours spread out to form a spectrum.

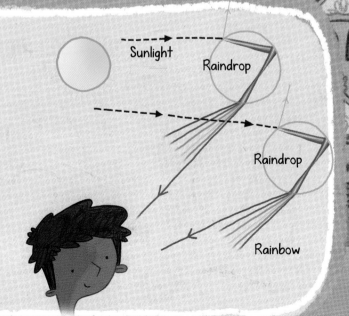

Sunlight

Raindrop

Raindrop

Rainbow

LIGHT BENDS

What creates a rainbow is the bending of light. Light bends when it travels from air into water because they are different materials. Imagine watching a fish in a pond. When light bouncing off the fish travels up towards your eye, it bends slightly when it leaves the water and enters the air. Your eye doesn't account for this, and so it thinks the light has just travelled in a straight line from the fish. This means your eye thinks the fish is shallower than it is.

RAINBOW FROM THE SKY

If you see a rainbow from up high, such as from an aeroplane, you'll be above the raindrops that create it. This means you're likely to see the rainbow as a full circle. On the ground, you only see the arc of a rainbow because that's what's visible above the horizon – the rest is hidden.

YOUR OWN MINI–RAINBOW

At certain times you can create a rainbow framed around your shadow. If you are high up on a misty mountainside, with the Sun directly behind you, your shadow will be projected down onto the mist below you. The Sun's light will be split into the colours of the rainbow when it hits the watery mist, and because you are above the water drops, you'll see the full rainbow circle. This cool effect is called a 'Brocken Spectre', or 'Mountain Spectre'!

FLOODING

Flooding happens when an area that is normally dry is covered in water. Sometimes, people choose to flood land, perhaps for farming, but often floods happen because of extreme weather and this causes major problems. People have had to deal with flooding disasters for many thousands of years. In the last 100 years alone, flooding has claimed millions of lives - more than any other natural disaster. Scientists say the biggest floods have a flow of water which is the same as the water from 40 Olympic-sized swimming pools gushing past every second!

ICE AGE MEGA—FLOOD

During the last ice age, between about 12,000 and 25,000 years ago, there was the most incredible deluge of water. This flood, named 'Missoula', ran for hundreds of kilometres through what is now the United States. Scholars think the flood began when a glacier slipped into a valley and blocked the natural flow of water. The water destroyed all in its path, and moved huge boulders, massing them into stacks hundreds of metres high! This makes the Missoula flood one of the biggest of all time.

WHEN MEASURING MEGA-FLOODS, WE FOCUS ON FRESHWATER, NOT OCEAN-BASED DELUGES OF WATER.

KURAY MEGA—FLOOD

Possibly the biggest flood in history happened in Russia. The Kuray was another Ice Age flood, and it is thought to have had surges the same as the volume of water in 6,800 olympic-sized pools flowing past every second!

FLOODS AT HOME

In many countries, certain areas of towns and cities are prone to flooding. Maybe because they are at the bottom of a hill where large amounts of rainfall can pool, or because they are next to a river with low banks. People living in these areas have to be flood aware and know how to use sandbags to stop floodwaters coming into their homes.

TOO MUCH RAIN

One mega-flood was actually caused by too much rain! It happened in 1953, in South America. It rained so much that the Amazon River overflowed at a vast rate. The Amazon River basin is the largest in the world, emptying 20% of the planet's freshwater into the oceans. Seasonal floods in the Amazon region are quite common, but 1953 was the largest meteorological (caused by rainfall) flood in recorded history and it resulted in a loss of life and homes.

VOLCANIC FLOOD POWER

About 10,000 years ago, in present-day Alaska, a volcano caused the Aniakchak flood. The volcanic eruption created a large crater, which became filled with rainwater over time. The water eroded the rim of the crater away and suddenly all that rainwater came flooding out at a rate of 400 Olympic-sized pools in one moment!

THE FUTURE OF WATER

Climate change today will have a big impact on the water cycle in the future. The natural cycles of the planet mean that Earth's climate is always changing (see page 110), but the difference today is that humans are also contributing to it. We've done this by burning too much fossil fuel such as coal and oil which pump carbon dioxide into the air – turn back to page 156 for a reminder about fossil fuels. Here are some of the challenges we are likely to face in the future, and ways we can help avoid them.

FLOODS

Climate change is causing the average global temperature to increase and 2016 was the hottest year ever recorded. The polar ice caps are shrinking. This will cause sea levels to rise, much heavier rainfall in some countries, and more flooding. Extreme flooding creates a new global problem – climate refugees. In 2005, a hundred people from Tegua, part of the island chain of Vanuatu, in the South Pacific, became the first ever climate change refugees. They had to be relocated to higher ground due to flooding linked to climate change.

DROUGHTS

In other parts of the globe, it is the lack of water which will be the problem of the future. Due to climate change, some areas are becoming drier and more difficult to live in. If there isn't enough water to support farming, crops won't grow. In poorer parts of the world, where people can't get food from elsewhere, this could lead to famine. Since 1970, it has been raining less in southern Africa, southern Asia, the Mediterranean and southwest America.

CUT THE CARBON

The good news is, there are lots of things you can do to tackle the water challenges we face. The main way to help our planet is for everyone to reduce their carbon emissions. By turning the lights off when you leave a room you'll use less electricity at home. If your family walk, cycle or take public transport rather than driving everywhere you'll reduce the amount of fuel used. Why not try growing your own fruit and vegetables as well, so they don't have to be transported around the world to reach you.

HOW TO SAVE WATER

Although much of the Earth's surface is covered in water, most of it is seawater rather than freshwater. No matter where in the world you live, there isn't a great deal of freshwater to go around. In fact, there's only 1% of freshwater available for humans and animals to drink and the world's population is growing! So help the planet by cutting down on the water you use.

Turn off the tap when you brush your teeth.

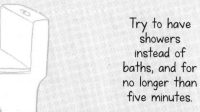

Try to have showers instead of baths, and for no longer than five minutes.

Toilet flushing uses the highest amount of water in a home, so don't flush unless you've actually used the toilet!

Ask an adult to fix any dripping taps about the house.

Don't do the washing up under a running tap – use the plug!

Collect rainwater for watering plants and washing the car.

A WATERY WORLD

With rising sea levels and more flash flooding, people will have to get their thinking caps on to adapt to a planet that is covered in even more water. We could become astronauts and build **colonies** on the Moon and Mars. Or we could become aquanauts and learn how to live underwater!

DEEP WATER TECH

Imagine if we could create underwater colonies and power them by harnessing the energy of water currents to generate renewable power. It's early days with underwater technology, but aquanaut scientists say that the technology to create huge underwater colonies actually already exists. Engineers still need to design better emergency evacuation systems and ways of storing larger water and air supplies to house more people, but we could be as little as 100 years away from some of us leaving the land and living in sea cities!

WATER BABIES

We may be more adaptable to life underwater than we think. On the west coast of Thailand there are tribes of people called the Moken. Moken children spend hours in the water every day, diving up and down, without their eyes becoming irritated. Remarkably, they have control of their eyes, just like seals and dolphins. They can make their pupils smaller and change the lens shape, which allows them to see clearly underwater. Other children of their age can't do this, nor can Moken adults. Scientists think it is largely down to practice. Perhaps more people in the future will be able to improve their natural underwater vision too?

AN AQUA-NAUT (LIKE AN ASTRO-NAUT, BUT UNDER WATER INSTEAD OF IN SPACE) IS AN UNDERSEA EXPLORER, ESPECIALLY ONE WHO WORKS OR LIVES UNDERWATER FOR LONG PERIODS OF TIME.

UNDERWATER HUMAN EVOLUTION

If we choose to explore our future underwater, we will have to adapt. But could aquanauts evolve enough to survive underwater unaided by technology? It's perfectly possible – over a few hundred thousand years! Plenty of other mammals live underwater and only come up for air every now and again – just look at whales and seals. But for the moment, the record for a person holding their breath underwater is just over 24 minutes. And we do NOT recommend you try this at home!

absorb To take in or soak up a substance.

altitude The height of a point in relation to the level of the ground or sea.

amplitude The distance from the highest or lowest point of a wave to its undisturbed position. The greater the amplitude, the louder the sound.

ancestor A person, usually further back than a grandparent, to whom you are related.

archaeology The study of human history by digging up the ground and examining the items found.

artefact An object made by a human that is of cultural or historical interest.

atmosphere The layers of gases surrounding planet Earth, and other planets.

atom The tiniest particle of any chemical element.

bacteria A group of tiny single-celled organisms, some of which cause disease.

bamboo A type of grass that is woody in appearance and grows very tall.

beacon A fire, or light, set up in a clear location to act as a warning or signal.

carbon A chemical element found in all living things on Earth.

cell The smallest unit from which all living organisms are made.

chasm A deep, narrow crack in the Earth's surface.

chemical A substance, relating to the study of chemistry.

chromosome A structure found in living cells which contains a coiled-up DNA molecule. Most human cells contain 23 pairs of chromosomes.

civilisation The society, culture and way of life of a group of people in a specific area.

climate The typical or average weather conditions in an area over a long period of time.

decibel A unit used to measure the loudness of a sound.

diversity A range of things, such as skin colour in humans.

DNA A huge molecule which contains all the information required for a living organism to live and grow.

drought A long period of unusually low rainfall that leads to a shortage of water in an area.

echo A sound caused by sound waves bouncing, or reflecting off a surface.

electricity A form of energy that can flow in a current, created by charged particles.

element A substance from which all matter is made and which can't be broken down into a simpler substance. Elements are grouped together in the periodic table.

energy The power to be active and perform tasks. It is not a substance but a resource.

entrepreneur A person who earns a living by setting up new businesses.

erosion The gradual destruction of something by nature; for example rock being worn away by wind and water.

estuary Where a river meets the sea and fresh water meets tidal sea water.

Eurasia The total continental landmass of Europe and Asia combined.

evaporate To turn from a liquid into a gas or vapour.

evidence The information that shows if something is real, true or valid.

evolve To develop gradually over time. Life on Earth evolved over billions of years.

famine Extreme shortage of food in a region.

fertile Rich soil or land where plants and crops grow successfully.

fossil The remains or imprint of a plant or animal found in rock that has been preserved for millions of years.

friction The resistance that one surface encounters when moving over another, causing it to slow down.

gas A fluid substance that will expand freely to fill any space.

gene DNA molecules are made up of thousands of sections called genes. Each gene in a living organism is a piece of information that controls how that organism looks or behaves. Genes are passed from parents to children.

generation All of the people born and living at around the same time.

geyser A hot spring in the ground that sends a tall column of water and steam into the air.

glacier A slow-moving, enormous mass of ice.

gravity The force that attracts an object towards the centre of the Earth and holds it on the surface or circling the planet, in orbit.

grazing Animals eating grass over a continuous period of time.

habitat The natural environment of a living organism.

hollow An object with a hole or empty space inside it, such as the bones of a bird or bat.

Ice Age A period in the Earth's history when the climate cooled and ice sheets spread across the planet.

inherit To receive a quality or characteristic from a parent or grandparent.

irrigation To supply water, typically in a channel, to land or crops to help them grow.

liquid A substance that flows freely.

livestock Farm animals.

locomotive A powered railway vehicle used to pull trains along.

magnetic An object that has an electrical charge and so attracts other objects towards it or pushes them away.

matter Physical substance in general.

medieval Relating to the period of time from roughly the 5th to the 15th centuries in Europe.

membrane A thin, flexible structure that acts as a lining or covering.

mineral A solid, naturally occurring substance made of one or more elements.

molecule A particle formed by a group of atoms bonded together that can take part in a chemical reaction.

molten A solid that has melted into a liquid due to high heat.

mythology A collection of stories, typically involving supernatural beings or events, belonging to a particular religious or cultural group.

native Where a person or living creature is from originally, even if they no longer live there.

nutrient A substance that provides nourishment to a living organism and allows it to grow.

GLOSSARY

orbit The curved path of an object around a star, planet or moon. The Earth orbits the Sun.

organic A substance relating to living matter.

organism A living animal, plant or single-celled life form.

oxygen A colourless, odourless gas found in the air.

palaeontology The area of scientific study that looks at fossils.

particle A tiny portion of matter.

pesticide A chemical used to destroy organisms that are harmful to farming crops.

pharaoh A ruler or king in ancient Egypt.

photosynthesis The process in plants that uses energy from sunlight to make sugar and oxygen from water and carbon dioxide.

piston A disc or short cylinder in a tube which moves up and down due to the force of a liquid or gas pressing against it. A piston creates motion in an engine.

plateau An area of fairly flat, high ground.

pollution A substance in the environment that has harmful or poisonous effects.

porous A material, usually rock, that has tiny holes in it through which liquid or air can pass or be soaked up.

predator An animal that naturally preys on another for food.

prehistory Time before written records began.

pressure A force applied to an object by something in contact with it.

protein An organic substance made from nutrients that is an essential part of all living organisms.

puberty The period during which children become adults.

pupil The dark, circular opening in the centre of the eye.

radioactive A substance that releases charged particles from itself.

rapids A fast-flowing choppy section of water in a river.

reaction A chemical process in which substances cause each other to change into different substances.

renewable A natural source of energy that is not reduced in amount when used, such as wind.

reservoir A large lake used to store and supply water.

silt Fine sand, clay and other materials carried by flowing water and then deposited in an area.

smelt To extract metal from its ore by heating and melting.

solid A substance that is firm and doesn't change its shape.

species A group of living organisms consisting of similar individuals, for example lions and tigers are both a species of cat.

vapour A solid or liquid substance held in the air, most commonly water.

vibrate To move continuously back and forth.

weathering To wear away or change the appearance of something through exposure to climate, weather and water.

INDEX

INDEX

253

FURTHER READING

If you'd like to find out more about planet Earth, how life evolved and the forces that shape our world, then here are some other books you might like to read:

Science Year by Year (Dorling Kindersley)
Packed with fascinating discoveries and facts, this illustrated timeline takes you on a fantastic journey through time, from stone tools and simple machines to space travel and robots.

How to Be a Space Explorer (Lonely Planet Kids)
Everything young explorers need to know to travel in space, covering what life in zero gravity is like, how to find your way around the solar system, and the all-important question of how to pee in a spacesuit!

Dinosaur Atlas (Lonely Planet Kids)
Travel back in time 150 million years. Open gatefolds and flaps to reveal lost prehistoric lands and the dinosaurs that once roamed them. Uncover the latest dinosaur discoveries and fascinating stories about how these ancient creatures lived.

Story of Life: Evolution (Big Picture Press)
A beautifully illustrated fold-out guide to evolution, starting with the first single-cell organisms and ending with modern life forms. Read it as a book or fold it all the way out.

Everything Volcanoes and Earthquakes (National Geographic Kids)
Incredible photos and amazing facts about the awesome powers of nature. Bursting with fascinating information about the biggest volcanic eruptions and earth-shattering earthquakes.

Everything Weather (National Geographic Kids)
Weather can be wild, freaky, and fascinating! Powerful twisters roar through homes; earthquakes shatter whole cities; hurricanes fly through towns. All you need to know about weather and all of its wildness will be found here.

Curious About Fossils (Smithsonian)
Explains why and where fossils form and looks at the colorful lives and important discoveries of some of the great early fossil hunters, as well as exploring modern fossil exploration and technology.

Eyewitness: Climate Change (Dorling Kindersley)
An in-depth look at global warming – what's causing it, what it might lead to and what we can do to fight back. With stunning photographs of the dramatic changes that are affecting the weather, the environment and us.

Ocean: A Children's Encyclopedia (Dorling Kindersley)
From the Arctic to the Caribbean, tiny plankton to giant whales, sandy beaches to the deepest depths, discover the mysterious world beneath the waves. Packed with fun graphics, interesting fact-boxes and high-quality photographs.

The Way Things Work Now (Dorling Kindersley)
A friendly woolly mammoth takes you on an incredible journey through the world of digital technology and explains how everything works.

Destination: Space (Wide Eyed Editions)
Just the thing if you want to explore the stars, planets and meteors in our galaxy, before launching into deep space and the galaxies beyond our own Milky Way.

What is Evolution? (Wayland)
How did life evolve from simple, single-celled creatures in the sea, to the amazingly complex and diverse creatures alive today? This book looks at how evolution has affected everything on Earth, over billions of years.

PLACES TO EXPLORE

From science museums to space centres, here are places you might like to visit. They have interactive experiments and experiences which are the perfect way to find out more. Have fun exploring!

UK

Science Museum, London
(www.sciencemuseum.org.uk)

Natural History Museum, London
(www.nhm.ac.uk)

National Space Centre, Leicester
(www.spacecentre.co.uk)

@Bristol, Bristol
(www.at-bristol.org.uk)

ThinkTank, Birmingham Science Museum, Birmingham
(www.birminghammuseums.org.uk/thinktank)

MAGNA, Rotherham
(www.visitmagna.co.uk/science-adventure)

Eureka, The National Children's Museum, Halifax
(www.eureka.org.uk)

Life Science Centre, Newcastle
(www.life.org.uk)

Glasgow Science Centre, Glasgow
(www.glasgowsciencecentre.org)

Aberdeen Science Centre, Aberdeen
(www.aberdeensciencecentre.org)

Techniquest, Cardiff
(www.techniquest.org)

W5, Belfast
(www.w5online.co.uk)

Australia

The Australian Museum, Sydney
(www.australianmuseum.net.au)

Sydney Observatory
(www.maas.museum/sydney-observatory)

Powerhouse Museum, Sydney
(www.maas.museum/powerhouse-museum)

Melbourne Museum, Melbourne
(www.museumvictoria.com.au/melbournemuseum)

Questacon, Canberra
(www.questacon.edu.au)

Sciencentre, Queensland Museum, Brisbane, Queensland
(www.sciencentre.qm.qld.gov.au)

USA

Liberty Science Center, Jersey City, New Jersey
(www.lsc.org)

Museum of Science & Industry, Chicago, Illinois
(www.msichicago.org)

Exploratorium, San Francisco, California
(www.exploratorium.edu)

Discovery Place Science, Charlotte, North Carolina
(www.discoveryplace.org)

Museum of Science, Boston, Massachusetts
(www.mos.org)

COSI, Columbus, Ohio
(www.cosi.org)

California Science Center, Los Angeles, California
(www.californiasciencecenter.org)

Smithsonian National Air and Space Museum, Washington, DC
(www.airandspace.si.edu)

The Franklin Institute, Philadelphia, Pennsylvania
(www.fi.edu)

California Academy of Sciences, San Francisco
(www.calacademy.org)

The Children's Museum of Indianapolis, Indianapolis, Indiana
(www.childrensmuseum.org)

Maryland Science Center, Baltimore, Maryland
(www.mdsci.org)

Carnegie Science Center, Pittsburgh, Pennsylvania
(www.carnegiesciencecenter.org)

Sci-Port Discovery Center, Shreveport, Louisiana
(www.sciport.org)

St Louis Science Center, St. Louis, Missouri
(www.slsc.org)

American Museum of Natural History, New York
(www.amnh.org)

Fernbank Museum of Natural History (www.fernbankmuseum.org) and Fernbank Science Center
(www.fernbank.edu)

Pacific Science Center, Seattle, Washington
(www.pacificsciencecenter.org)

Science Museum of Minnesota, St Paul, Minnesota (www.smm.org)

Gulf Coast Exploreum Science Center, Mobile, Alabama
(www.exploreum.com)

Union Station, Kansas City, Missouri
(www.unionstation.org/sciencecity)

Montshire Museum of Science, Norwich, Vermont (www.montshire.org)

The Discovery Science Place, Tyler, Texas (www.discoveryscienceplace.org)

Museum of Discovery and Science, Fort Lauderdale, Florida (www.mods.org)

OMSI, Portland, Oregon (www.omsi.edu)

Arizona Science Center, Phoenix, Arizona (azscience.org)

PICTURE CREDITS

The publisher would like to thank the following for their kind permission to reproduce their photographs:

(Key: b-bottom; c-centre; l-left; r-right; t-top)

Earth

Getty: Chris Clor 10; Arctic-Images 14; Paul Chesley 26; Salvator Barki 27; Phil Mislinski / Stringer 28; JONATHAN NOUROK 33; Dk Fotography / EyeEm 37; Glowimages 39; Nico Tondini 41; Violetastock 45; Yury Prokopenko 49; Nigel Pavitt 56-57; ALEXANDER JOE 57; UniversalImagesGroup 65 (l).

Shutterstock: www.sandatlas.org 18 (l); Tyler Boyes 18 (r); elenaburn 19; Lyudmila Suvorova 32-33; shootmybusiness 42; Ruud Morijn Photographer 62-63; seb001 65 (r).

Air

Getty: Daniel J. Cox 78-79; Daniel J. Cox 79 (l); Wild Horizon 80; Print Collector 81; Tim Graham 86-87; Peter Bischoff / Stringer 89; U.S. Navy 90; Bruce Bennett / Staff 90-91; Education Images 109 (t); Marcos Welsh 109 (b); Gilles Mingasson 111; Space Frontiers 112; Alexander Nicholson 112-113; REG WOOD 123 (t).

Shutterstock: Jens Mayer 79 (cl); Daniel Schreiber 79 (cr); Travfi 79 (r); phdwhite 84-85; Amelandfoto 104; Tomas Kotouc 105; Zhao jian kang 121; Janelle Lugge 123 (b).

Fire

Getty: NZPIX 130-131; Andrea Pistolesi 138-139; William West 145; Chris Pusey 149; Pauline Bernard/EyeEm 150-151; Johner Images 152-153; Amanda Hart 153 (t); Dave King 153 (b); Richard Nichols/EyeEm 160-161; Danita Dellimont/Gallo Images 160 (b); DEA/A. Dagli Orti/De Agostini Picture Library 161 (t); Geoff Dan 161 (cr); DEA/A. De Gregorio/De Agostini Picture Library 161 (b); Marcelo Horn 166-167; Tetra Images/Dan Bannister 166 (r); Kevin Schafer 167 (t); Underwood Archives/Archive Photos 168 (b); Print Collector/Hulton Archive 169 (bc); Roger Viollet Collection 169 (br); Ben Osborne/The Image Bank 170-171; Imagevixen/RooM 175; Ian Cuming/IKon Images 176-177; Lester Lefkowitz 176 (c); Chris Sattlberger/Blend Images 177; Tass 178 (b); Photography of Beauty and Mystery 179.

Shutterstock: FloridaStock 174; Ververidis Vasilis 178-179; Sebastien Burel 180-181.

Water

Getty: Anton Petrus 200; Tan Yilmaz 201; Hugo 210-211; oversnap 224 (tl); DEA / PUBBLI AER FOTO/Contributor 224 (tr); manx_in_the_world 224 (bl); CampPhoto 224 (br); AAAAAAAAAA AAAAAAAA 225 (tl); Daan Steeghs / EyeEm 225 (tr); Kirill Kukhmar (cl); Duniel Arantes 225 (cr); Michael Gottschalk 225 (bl); macroworld 228-229; Joe Raedle 228 (l); Sue Flood 228 (r); Enrique R Aguirre Aves 229 (t); Mint Images - Frans Lanting 229 (b); CHRIS ROUSSAKIS 233 (tl); Arterra 233 (c); PhotoAlto/Jerome Gorin 233 (bl); Rolf Hicker 238 (t); Hans-Peter Merten 238 (c); Naufal MQ 238 (b); Robin Smith 239 (tl); Adventure_Photo 239 (tr); VW Pics 239 (b); VCG 242-243; Archive Photos / Stringer 243; Images Etc Ltd 244.

Shutterstock: beboy 205; DNSokol 225; patjo 232 (t); Suprun Vitaly 232 (b); Andrey Armyagov 233 (br); Kelly Headrick 237; photopulse 241.